PREACHING THAT EMPOWERS GOD'S PEOPLE

Other Books:

THE Minister's Handbook: *A Guide for Leadership*

Conducting Church Audits: *A Guide for Internal Auditors*

A Pastor's Introduction to Church Administration:
Administering the 21st Century Church Effectively

SECOND EDITION

PREACHING THAT EMPOWERS GOD'S PEOPLE:
Expository Preaching in the 21st Century

JEREMY W. ODOM

©2016

Preaching that Empowers God's People, 2nd edition
Copyright © 2016 by Jeremy W. Odom
All rights reserved.

ISBN: 978-0-9970-9561-6

Published by Big O Publishing Group
Natchitoches, Louisiana

No part of this publication may be reproduced, stored in a retrieval system, or transmitted in any form or by any means, electronic, mechanical, photocopying, recording, or otherwise, without the prior permission of the copyright owner, except for brief quotations included in a review of the book.

The author has worked to ensure that all information in this book is accurate as of the time of publication. As research and practice advance, however, standards may change. For this reason it is recommended that readers evaluate the applicability of any recommendations in light of particular situations and changing standards.

Big O Publishing Group has made every effort to trace the ownership of all quotes. In the event of a question arising from the use of a quote, we regret any error made and will be pleased to make the necessary correction in future printings and editions of this book.

Library of Congress Control Number 2015920219

Printed in the United States of America

Contents

Preface i
Dedication iii
About the Author v
Chapter 1 Critical Condition 1
Chapter 2 Biblical Discernment 13
Chapter 3 Homiletics 39
Chapter 4 What Is Expository Preaching 55
Chapter 5 The Need for Expository Preaching 69
Chapter 6 Exegesis & Expository Preaching 81
Chapter 7 Creating the Expository Sermon 97
Chapter 8 Varieties of Expository Sermons 123
Chapter 9. Expository Context 135
Chapter 10 Effective Delivery 143
Chapter 11 Sermon Do's and Don'ts 157
Appendix 1 167
Appendix 2 175
Notes 179
References 183
INDEX 187

Preface

What is a good sermon?

It has been taught through seminaries across the land that the main tenet of a good sermon is the development of a good introduction and conclusion; then keeping the two close together. I would argue however that in order for a sermon to be good, it must be biblical in nature.

All across America, preachers are being encouraged to return the fine art of expository preaching. Having been encompassed by great orators such as Charles Spurgeon, E.K. Bailey and Dr. Martin Luther King, Jr., the church cannot afford to continue its allowance of lazy preparation in its pulpits.

This project was undertaken with the goal of identifying the lost art of expository preaching and encouraging its use in the 21st century church. The correct use of expository preaching offers a plethora of benefits to both the expositor and preacher.

By implementing the expository sermon into our repertoire of sermons, we undertake the commitment to transforming lives of men into empowered people of God. This can only be accomplished through the correct exegesis of the Scripture.

Although not an all-inclusive book of exposition, the surface of the subject matter has been scratched and this book will lend to the reader valuable resources.

JEREMY W. ODOM, D.DIV.
PROFESSOR OF CHRISTIAN MINISTRY
SOUTHERN CHRISTIAN BIBLE COLLEGE
March 7, 2016

In Humble Submission

Dedication

This book is dedicated to
Preachers and Pastors everywhere
Keep watch of the flock!

To my beloved Pastor and Mentor
Dr. Mitchell C. Herndon, Sr.
Thank you. Without your support and counsel,
I would have never finished this book.

In memory of my seminary instructors
Rev. G. Stanley Lewis & Rev. Joseph D. Dupree, D.Th.
Thank you. I will never forget your wise instruction.

About the Author

Dr. Jeremy W. Odom is the General President of the Louisiana Ministerial Association, Inc. He is a Professor of Christian Ministry at the Southern Christian Bible College and Seminary where he also serves as Dean. He also serves as the Chairman of the Board of Trustees for the National Pastors and Ministers Conference.

Dr. Odom acknowledges being called into the Gospel Ministry at the tender age of six while attending Damascus Missionary Baptist Church of Lena, Louisiana under the leadership of Rev. William Batts. However, Dr. Odom did not preach his Apprenticeship Sermon until the age of fifteen at the First Baptist Church Amulet of Natchitoches under the guidance of Rev. Dr. Joseph D. Dupree.

Dr. Odom has served in the Gospel Ministry in many various positions. He has served as a Youth Pastor, Assistant Pastor, Senior Evangelist, Elder, Prison Chaplain and eventually Senior Pastor. His ministry has been heard all across America and in combat areas of Iraq.

Dr. Odom is the author of several books that are currently being utilized by seminaries, Bible students, preachers, teachers and scholars worldwide.

Dr. Odom has earned countless awards, including those from President of the United States, Department of the Army, Mayor of Natchitoches and Who's Who? He is a member of the Prince Hall Free & Accepted Masons hailing from Dawn of Light Lodge #22 in Natchitoches, LA. In 2012, he was awarded the Honorary Doctorate of Divinity from the American Bible University.

A native of Natchitoches, Louisiana, Dr. Odom has been licensed to preach since 2002 and an ordained minister since 2008. He currently serves as an Associate Minister of the First Baptist Church-North of Natchitoches, LA under the divine leadership of Dr. Mitchell C. Herndon, Sr.

Chapter 1 Critical Condition

Pulpits across America in the 21st Century Church are being faced with the dilemma of attempting to keep the attention of the pews on the Word of God. Many of the centuries great orators could attest that it's all in how you tell them. Unfortunately for many, our sermons are in serious critical condition.

Losing People in Your Sermons

Are you losing people when you preach? Do people check out during your sermons? After listening to thousands of sermons and preaching quite a few of them, I have learned some different ways which preachers lose people in their sermons.

1. Sloppy Transitions
   You just told a great story. It was funny and thought-provoking. But as soon as the story ended you suddenly switched direction and started talking about something else. Wait... what? Slow down. How did we get from that funny thing your kid did to some old guy in the Old Testament? Where is the connection?

   You have to make clear connections between one part of your sermon and next. Otherwise people get lost in the transition. It is as simple as saying, "that funny thing my kid did reminds me of a story in the Old Testament where a man named Samuel experienced something similar."

Boom, Bridge built. Transition made. I see where you are going. Typical transition points are after the introduction, before and after scripture, before and after illustrations, and before the conclusion. Please don't overlook how important a simple transition statement is in keeping everyone in the audience on track with you.

2. Too Many Points
   I recently sat in on a sermon where the preacher has so many different points with many different fill-in-the-blanks that I got lost. I seriously had no idea what exactly this man was talking about, because his points were all lover the map.

   Sure, they were all good points, but I lost the point in all the points. Keep it simple. What is the big, overarching idea that people need to understand from the passage of scripture?

   Stick to one point or at least one main point or will lose people.

   HINT: When your sub-points have sub-points, there is a good chance you are getting a little carried away.

3. TMI (Too Much Information)
   When you introduce scripture you become a historian. You describe the architecture, the types of clothing people wore, the political climate, and every last ounce of the historical detail you can. Yes, you did your homework. Yes, you are thorough. But most people, frankly, do not care.

Give people just enough information to set up the scripture and then let scripture speak on its own. Only give details if it is essential to understanding the meaning of the text. You will have to explain some historical situations or nuances of the time period, but don't get carried away.

If you take too long setting up a passage of scripture, you will lose people. This is a sermon, not a history class. Your goal should be to point people to the Bible, not prove how smart you are.

4. Long Introductions
   Get to the point. Introductions that take forever make people's minds wander to lunch or Fantasy Football. I don't care if you have a great story. Get to the point.

   What are you talking about? Why should I care? How does this impact me? These are questions people in the congregation want to know. You will lose people if you ramble for ten minutes before they have a clue what you are going to preach about.

5. Lazy Conclusions
   Like an airplane your sermon began with a smooth takeoff. The flight was good. But when it came time to land, you crashed. Consistent with the airplane analogy, there are two types of lazy conclusions.

   a. **Circling the runway**
      You know it is time to end the sermon, but you aren't exactly sure how to end it so you keep summarizing things you already said. HINT: If you said "In conclusion..." and then preached

another 10-15 minutes, you are probably circling the runway.

    b. **Abrupt landing**
You said everything you planned on saying. You ran out of material. It is now time to end the sermon so you immediately say, "Let's Pray." Although this approach may be better than circling the runway, your awkward conclusion failed to capitalize on one of the most important parts of the sermon.

A good conclusion should be a smooth landing. As you descend, summarize what you talked about, challenge the audience again to do something with what they heard, and have a memorable closing statement.

The closing statement may be a phrase you have repeated throughout the message, a scripture, a quote, a story, a challenge, or whatever else fits.

Remember, the last thing you say in a sermon is often the most memorable. Pay attention to this, so you don't leave everyone with, "Well, umm... that's all I have today. So...let's pray."

6. Abstract Thoughts Without Real-Life Application
You preach a lot of big ideas, abstract concepts, and sound doctrine. That's great. But even the best doctrinal teaching without real-life application will bore the snot out of most church-goers.

The whole time you are painting a theological masterpiece, they are asking, "So what? How does that affect me?" Selfish?--Yes, but true nonetheless. So go ahead and keep on preaching abstract thoughts and concepts, but don't stop there. Answer the questions you know they are asking.

Say, "So what? How does this impact you and me? ..." Then launch into some seriously detailed, concrete, real-world application. Not only will your people appreciate the practical tips, they will begin to appreciate theology more as they see hot actually does matter.

7. Preaching Too Long
I will probably get some pushback here, and that is OK. But it is a rare thing to find a preacher who can hold an audience captive for more than an hour. Yes, there are some who do it well, but do their people really love it or just tolerate it?

Personally, if I am sitting in on a sermon that begins to go over 30 minutes my attention begins to drift. And I'm a preacher who loves listening to preaching! I have to consciously refocus myself on the message.

Most people struggle listening to one person talk for longer than 30 minutes, especially if they are not auditory learners. It had better be really entertaining (like a great comedian), or incredibly impactful (insert memory of the best sermon you have ever hear here).

Personally, I would rather leave the audience wanting more preaching than less. This may just be my opinion, but if you are a long-winded preacher, I challenge you to test this. Take a survey of random people in your church. Ask for honest feedback on the length of your sermons. (Want truly honest results? Have someone other than a staff member to conduct the survey for you.)

8. Christian Words Without Explanations
If you are saying a lot of words like "Sanctification," "Transubstantiation," "Regeneration," "Incarnation," or any other term you learned in seminary, you are losing people. HINT: if there is an "ation" in the word, you better define it or pick a different word.

Don't make people feel like they need a dictionary or a seminary degree to understand what you are talking about. Even words that you might think are common knowledge need proper explanation. What you think of when saying "sin" and other people think you mean could be two very different things. Define your terms.

Go ahead and use these technical terms if you want, but explain what you mean in simple terms every time or you will lose people. This may get a little tiresome for you, because you already know what you are talking about. But you cannot assume that everyone in the congregation is on the same page (because most of them probably aren't).

Keys to Preaching a Lousy Sermon

Most people, when they preach, want to do well right?

Most people want others to experience God, encounter truth, and leave changed. Most people want the hard work they put into their sermons to have some sort of impact on the people listening.

Some people aim to preach a lousy sermon. If you'd like to be one of those preachers, here's your list.

1. Spend very little time praying.
   If your sermon is going to be lousy, this is where you've got to start. Don't seek God in prayer. Don't spend time begging Him to lead your thoughts and your words. Don't plead with him to soften hard hearts and open blind eyes.

2. Make your sermon purely about "teaching" propositional truths.
   Go at it like your 7th grade history teacher... the one that you thought was boring. You know the one that you didn't remember anything from her class. Just teach lofty moral platitudes and propositional truth statements that don't drive any application home. That'll get the job done.

3. Make your "study time" primarily about listening to other preachers talk about that passage.
   Whatever you do, don't read the Bible for yourself and study the Scriptures to show yourself approved (2 Timothy 2:15). Live off of *others'* relationship with God, their experience with Him, and the knowledge and insight *they've* gained.

4. Don't use the word "I" at all.
   Don't let things get too personal. Use 'they' and 'them' primarily. Slip in a few 'you people' and you're good to go. Talk about "those people" a lot.

5. Heap burden after burden on top of your people.
   Condemnation is the way to go. Try to make sure those condemning thoughts weave themselves throughout your sermon. Something like 'The 5 ways you sinned this week and didn't know it' or 'Why God hates you' or 'The 17 ways you'll never measure up" or "Quit trying...you're not doing any good any way."

6. Be sure to yell. Loudly. And obnoxiously.
   Be careful with this one, though. People might think that, because you're yelling, you're saying something important. We all know you're not. Just be careful.

7. Be completely absent and disengaged from people the entire week leading up to your sermon.
   Your ministry of loving and serving people could bleed over into your sermon if you're not careful. The times you spend praying with and for people could have a drastic impact on the way you teach and preach. Be careful.

8. Don't ask for anyone else's input prior to preaching.
   Study, prepare, write, and rehearse on your own. Don't let anyone else take a look at your notes, your wording, or the direction you're going to head on Sunday. Go it alone, my friend. Nobody else is as awesome as you are. The moment someone else tries to offer you a bit of advice, refer back to #6, above.

9. Don't spend time wrestling through your own sins and weaknesses.
   Just focus on other people. It's much easier this way. Focusing on your self gets all personal. And it means you have to be vulnerable. And...well, I'll stop right

there. I was just about to go into confession time. I can't go there...and neither can you.

There you go. Nine steps to preaching a lousy sermon. Now get out there and start preaching!

Stealing Sermons

A church wrote this particular blog saying that they have discovered their pastor was preaching sermons from their website virtually verbatim. When the church confronted their pastor about it, he didn't notice anything wrong. I am not aware of the pastor or church, but I do have some friendly observations.

1. The nature of the Internet makes it easy to steal someone else's work and make it your own.
2. But the Internet also makes it very easy to find out when a pastor has been using someone else's work.
3. There are several websites that off full text sermons online, knowing that pastors around the world will use them in their own message preparation.
4. Having served as pastor and leader of a statewide ecumenical association, I know how hectic and pressured life can be. Some weeks all your study time disappears because you are dealing with one crisis after another. The picture of a pastor spending 30 uninterrupted hours in his study each week is more a myth than a reality. Especially in smaller churches, the pastor inevitably gets pulled in a dozen directions each week. In larger churches a pastor probably has staff members who care for various needs in the congregation. But in smaller churches, the pastor may be the only person on staff so it all tends to fall on him.

5. Most churches would not object to a pastor occasionally leaning heavily on the work of others. Life happens in unpredictable ways. But if those unpredictable things keep on happening and you keep preaching the sermons of John Piper, John MacArthur, Herschel Ford, W.A. Criswell, Joseph Parker and Charles Spurgeon, you will be found out sooner or later.
6. Usually he is found out because the preacher doesn't sound like himself. Spurgeon had an amazing gift for painting word pictures. I doubt that any of us today could successfully preach exactly as he did in London 130 years ago. Times have changed, expectations are different, and the culture of the 21st century is quite different from late-19th-century London. But Spurgeon's sermons remain a treasure of sermonic gold that every preacher should mine.
7. I know of one pastor who preached a series that sounded so unlike his normal preaching that people went away scratching their heads, saying, "Where did he get that?" Now I don't know where he got it, but it sounded so unlike his normal preaching that people noticed the difference and commented on it.
8. Having said all that, if you are preaching through a book of the Bible, there is nothing more valuable than reading a book of expository sermons. That's where the Internet can be very useful. Some years ago when I was preaching through Genesis 1-11, within the space of two hours I downloaded over a hundred sermons (all free) from preachers around the world, all on Genesis 1-11. As I worked through the text, I found it very useful to see how others had handled the same material.
9. There is a fine line that a preacher must not cross, and it's hard to say exactly where that line is. For instance, I enjoy John Piper and read his sermons

almost every week, always with profit. I have used material from his sermons on different occasions, but I don't preach his sermons because (besides all the obvious reasons) they are his sermons, not mine. They don't sound like me and I don't sound like him. I use quotes, illustrations and ideas from all sorts of places, but I make them my own. Or I set them apart with quotes. Or I rephrase them. Or I just throw them into the "homiletical juicer" and let them ferment for a while.

10. What about using an outline verbatim? From my point of view, that's fine because an outline is not a sermon, it's more the skeleton. I don't think you need to give credit for an outline unless it is amazingly unique. The same holds true for ideas and thoughts that you may find here and there. No one wants to hear a sermon that sounds like a pastiche of quotes: "As John Piper pointed out...John MacArthur suggested this application...Spurgeon used this illustration...To borrow a thought from Geoff Thomas..." Some of this is just a matter of common sense. When you borrow a big section or a very unique idea and certainly when there is a significant quote, give the attribution. But don't go overboard either.

11. What about the pastor who allegedly uses the sermons online verbatim? That's just plain dumb. Dumb, dumb, dumb.

12. In earlier years I used to say that people could use my sermons any way they like, and I still mean that. But I never meant, "Use them word for word." It never occurred to me that someone would do that. You are bound to get caught sooner or later.

13. So this is what I say nowadays: You are welcome to use my sermons in your own message preparation.

Use them, amend them, revise them, by all means improve them, and make them your own.
14. I would normally hesitate to speak for a great man like C.H. Spurgeon, but I think he would agree with me on this count.
15. Don't preach anyone else's sermon verbatim.
16. Bottom line:

Milk many cows but make your own butter.

Chapter 2 Biblical Discernment

In its simplest definition, discernment is nothing more than the ability to decide between truth and error, right and wrong. Discernment is the process of making careful distinctions in our thinking about the truth. In other words, the ability to think with discernment is synonymous with an ability to think biblically. First Thessalonians 5:21-22 and 1 John 4:1 teaches that is the responsibility of every Christian to be discerning. According to the New Testament, discernment is not optional for the believer-it is required.

The mission of the church is to preach the gospel and make disciples. Additionally it is to be "the pillar and support of the truth" (1 Tim. 3:15). That's why Paul says that Elders must "hold fast the faithful word which is in accordance with the teaching, that [they] may be able both to exhort in sound doctrine and to refute those who contradict" (Titus 1:9)."

That requires discernment, which enables us to progress in righteousness and protects us from sin and error (Phil. 1:9-11). If discernment is lacking, we can fall prey to the kinds of errors, confusion, and spiritual excesses that plague so many churches today (some of which we will address in this chapter).

The key to living an uncompromising life lies in one's ability to exercise discernment in every area of his or her life. For example, failure to distinguish between truth and error leaves the Christian subject to all manner of false teaching. False teaching then leads to an unbiblical mindset, which results in unfruitful and disobedient living-a certain recipe for compromise.

I am afraid that in many quarters of modern Christianity we are losing sight not only of our *distinctions* as a Christian community, but also our *essentials*. Rather than taking a strong, united stand on orthodox doctrine, we are being pressured to pare back to the lowest common denominator for the sake of "harmony and unity within the Body of Christ." This chapter will focus on four key elements of discernment:

- The definition of discernment
- The call to discernment
- The path to discernment
- The need for discernment

I. Defining Discernment

PRIMARY GREEK TERMS

Each of these Greek words speaks of exercising one's critical faculties as directed by the Holy Spirit and instructed by God's Word.

1. *Anakrino* – To distinguish, or separate out so as to investigate; to examine, scrutinize, question; to hold a preliminary judicial examination preceding the trial proper. (Illustration Acts 17:11)

2. *Diakrino* – To separate, discriminate; to learn by discriminating; to determine, decide. (Illustration 1 Cor. 11:29-30)

3. *Diakrisis* – A distinguishing, a clear discrimination, discerning, judging. (Examples 1 Cor. 12:10; Heb. 5:14)

4. *Kritikos* – Translated "judge." Means "fit for, or skilled in, judging (from which the English word

"critical" is derived); "discriminating and passing judgment on the thoughts and feelings." (Illustration: Heb. 4:12)

PRACTICAL, WORKING DEFINITIONS
This kind of discernment differs from the Spiritual Gift of the distinguishing of spirits (1 Cor. 12:8, 10). Distinguishing of spirits is a particular gift given to some in the early church for the purpose of identifying the source of prophetic utterances (e.g., Peter with Ananias and Sapphira); whereas discernment is something *every believer* is to develop.

1. *Jay Adams*
Discernment is "the ability to distinguish God's thoughts and God's ways from all others.

2. *John MacArthur*
It is the "ability to understand, interpret, and apply truth skillfully. . . . Authentic spiritual discernment must begin with Scripture-revealed truth"

3. *Summary definition*
Discernment is the ability to distinguish truth from error, righteousness from unrighteousness, through the skillful application of biblical principles.

II. The Call to Discernment
Proverbs 2:1-6; Philippians 1:9-11; Hebrews 5:11-14; 1 John 4:1-3

1. The level of our discernment will determine the level of our ability to approve what is excellent, which in turn determines our:

- Sincerity in the faith
- Blamelessness in Christian living
- Fruit of righteousness
- The glory and praise we bring to God

2. This is no casual or optional matter; it is Christianity at its core.

III. The Path to Discernment

The path to greater discernment is fourfold:

- **Know the Lord** (1 Corinthians 2:14-16) Paul says that the Spirit-led and indwelt believer understands spiritual things, but he himself is not understood by unbelievers.

- **Know the Word** (Heb. 4:12) The Word is the MODEL AND BASIS for proper discernment. Incidentally, to know the Word, you must put time into it.

- **Apply the Word** (1 John 2:12-14). Those who are strong in the Word have the doctrinal fortitude and discernment to overcome Satan; because Satan's primary assaults are in the area of doctrine.

- **Test all things** (1 John 4:1-3; 1 Thess. 5:20-21). That doesn't mean to constantly be suspicious, but don't accept something as from God unless it passes the test of Scripture.

IV. The Need for Discernment

Factors contributing to a deficient discernment:
- **Tares in the Church**
    - Tares are unbelievers (Matthew 13:24-30)

- Unbelievers cannot discern spiritual truth.
- When unbelievers are present in the church, the corporate ability of the church to discern God's will and ways can suffer, especially if unbelievers are in positions of influence (through relationships, finances, or positions of spiritual authority).
- That's one reason we must maintain a high standard for leaders.

- **Ignorance**
  - Ignorance of sound doctrine
    By ignorance, I don't mean stupidity, but lack of knowledge of biblical doctrines due to immaturity in the Word or neglect of the Word.

    a. Immaturity in the Word
       Perhaps you're a new believer. You aren't neglecting the Word; you simply haven't had time to grow in your understanding of biblical principles.

    b. Neglect of the Word
       1) This is willful ignorance as opposed to immaturity.

       2) This may involve the erroneous idea that we are not responsible for biblical principles we don't know, even though we've had opportunity to learn them. (1 Corinthians 3:1-3; Romans 10:1; Hebrews 5:11-14 are strong re-

bukes to people who should have known better, but were spiritually and doctrinally inattentive and their failure to grow in the Word brought serious consequences.)

- Ignorance of what others believe
  a. Sometimes we simply <u>don't know what others teach</u>, or we <u>refuse to believe they actually believe what they teach</u>.

    - Therefore we might unwittingly think they are Christians.

    - Or support them financially, or even pray for their efforts. (2 John 5-11)

    - It's a serious thing to support or otherwise encourage the activities of non-Christian religious teachers. In doing so we:
        o Violate Christian love
        o Participate in their sin
        o Lose a full reward
        o Lose ground on what the gospel has accomplished.

  b. Example:
    - I hear many Christians speak fondly of the Roman Catholic Church as if the differences between Catholicism and

Protestantism were merely matters of worship format or incidental doctrines.

- I am speaking here of Catholicism as a doctrinal system, not of individual Catholics.

- I am addressing their *theology*: what they believe about salvation, the Bible, and other doctrines that so many people believe we hold in common.

c. The Roman View of Salvation
   1) Salvation is <u>not</u> by faith alone. The Catholic Church maintains that if you believe that salvation is by faith alone, *<u>you are damned</u>*!

   2) Salvation requires good works.

   3) Salvation requires personal punishment for sins.

   4) Salvation requires the sacrament of baptism. In Catholic theology a sacrament is a means by which someone receives sanctifying grace. That's why we identify baptism as *ordinance* rather than a *sacrament*. The Council of Trent also declared that the *instrumental* cause of justification (the means by which it is obtained) is

not faith, but "the sacrament of baptism.

    5) Salvation is through union with the Catholic Church

d. The Roman view of Scripture
The documents of the Second Vatican Council affirm that "it is not from sacred Scripture alone that the [Catholic] Church draws her certainty about everything which has been revealed," But "sacred tradition [transmits] in its full purity God's word which was entrusted to the apostles."

    1) How do we harmonize that with our belief that Scripture itself is the sole binding rule of faith and practice for all Christians? The answer is obvious: we can't!

    2) On what basis then do we establish common ground for ministry? It can't be on the basis of the gospel or of the source of spiritual authority.

e. Someone may object:
"But I grew up in the Catholic Church and I don't believe that. And I know lots of Catholics who don't believe that."

1) But the point is Catholicism teaches it!

2) Salvation = faith in Christ *plus* baptism.

3) Gal. 1 – That strikes at the very heart of evangelical Christianity.

f. What's the point?

    a. We have a religious movement that claims to be Christian yet has a gospel of faith plus works, which is exactly what Romans, Galatians and Colossians were written to refute.

    b. We have a religious movement that attacks the sufficiency of Scripture by adding church tradition and special revelations through the Pope. When the Mormons do that the Book of Mormon, we cry "cult" and take all precautions to avoid them. When Jehovah's Witnesses do that with their New World Translation and supposed revelations of the end of the world, we cry "cult" and take all precautions to avoid them.

c. Why it is when the Catholics do it, many Christians embrace them as true brothers and sisters in Christ, and unite with them in various ecumenical efforts?

   d. These are the Christian essentials that are at stake, not merely denominational distinctive.

- **Spiritual Pride**
1. By spiritual pride I mean an unwillingness to learn from those with greater knowledge and discernment than ourselves.

2. This is an important point because those with the least discernment often are the most vocal about issues in the church.

   a. But their positions, if not grounded in discerning application of God's Word, must be based on <u>something less</u> (i.e., emotions, experience, prejudice, preference, ignorance, pride).

   b. This is usually where the most serious problems arise in an otherwise solid congregation.

- **Settling for a "Simple Faith"**
1. What I <u>*don't*</u> mean
   a. By "Simple Faith" I do not mean a new or immature faith that is in the process of growing.

b. I believe in the brand of simple faith that says "God said it, I believe it, that settles it!" But not the kind that attempts to mask spiritual neglect or laziness. That is unbiblical and detrimental to discernment and spiritual maturity.

2. What I *do* mean
I mean a spiritual laziness or unwillingness to increase one's biblical knowledge or depth of commitment to the things of God.

3. An apparent attitude
Some Christians convey the attitude that Christianity is somehow more noble or preferable when uncluttered by doctrinal depth or disciplined training in the Word, or that those who are deeper in the things of the Lord are somehow out of step with reality or in some spiritual ivory tower.

   a. That simply isn't true! Every true believer has the mind of Christ (1 Cor. 2) and is responsible for developing their capacity to discern spiritual things.

   b. God's Word is to be at the center of our lives and thinking (Deut. 6:4-9)

   c. Psalms 119:97-100 - **No Seminary training there!** Just diligent meditation on God's Word, which He infuses with spiritual wisdom and insight.

   d. As we gather each week and devote ourselves to worship, fellowship, and Bible study, we are involved in a sacred and never-ending process:

- It's the process of <u>renewing your mind</u> that Paul speaks of in Romans 12:2.

- For example, you come and perhaps the Sunday school lesson doesn't really grab you, or the sermon just doesn't seem to speak to your heart or need, but the process of building discernment, wisdom, and insight is still processing one step at a time.

- You are systematically increasing the reservoir of biblical knowledge that the Holy Spirit will use to instruct, encourage, and transform you step by step (2 Cor. 3:18)

- Those who neglect the discipline of worship and instruction, or deceive themselves by thinking they have all the biblical data they need in life, are missing the point.

- We do it because we Love the God of the Word

    - Because we are commanded to do so (2 Tim. 2:15)

- Because we want to be fully equipped for every good work (2 Tim. 3:16-17).
- Because we want to overcome the evil one (1 John 2:12)

    1 John 2:12 - Spiritual young men have overcome him because they are strong in the Word. The enemy is very sophisticated and comes as <u>*an angel of light*</u>. We must be prepared. Our lives constantly bombarded by the influences of Satan's evil world system. Therefore we must be diligent to saturate ourselves with the things of God if we expect to overcome the world and progress on godliness.

4. Blind loyalty
    By blind loyalty I mean the fallacy that you are not responsible for your theological errors if your leaders lead you astray.

    a. It's true that leaders bear the primary responsibility.
    b. However, that does not relieve their followers of responsibility also.
    c. Matthew 15:14 & Matthew 23:15

5. "No shame" exemption?
   The idea of a simple faith can also include the fallacy that 2 Timothy 2:15 applies only to ministers, and that "regular Christians" are exempt. We've already seen that each Christian is personally responsible for their devotion to Christ and His Word.

- **Experience**

Obviously there can be great value in personal experience, although it must conform to Scripture and not vice versa. Scripture must govern our experiences. Personal experience alone is not to be the determiner of biblical truth. Discernment will drive us to the Word to evaluate each and every situation.

1. Many professing Christians seem to elevate personal experience over biblical doctrine, as if experience were the primary means of determining what is from God.

2. This is perhaps the greatest challenge facing the contemporary church.

3. More and more people are taking the position that if someone supposedly has a personal experience with God, we must never question or criticize it. Criticism (testing claims against Scripture) is seen as disrespectful, narrow-minded, dogmatic, and insensitive.

4. God *never* allows experience to interpret or stand in judgment on His Word. And for good reason. Our senses can be deceived through an experience.

5. Rather than relying on experience, we are to test all things, then cling tenaciously to what <u>is</u> good and true—not what <u>seems</u> true, or what <u>we hope</u> is true, what <u>might be</u> true, or what <u>feels true</u> because of some experience we've had (1 Thess. 5:21).

6. Perhaps the most powerful example of building one's theology on experience (sometimes called experiential theology) is the Charismatic Movement.

   a. One common experience (tongues) unites professing believers from many different denominational and doctrinal perspectives.

   b. Just consider what doctrines have to be jettisoned for Catholics, Anglicans, Episcopalians, Presbyterians, Lutherans, Pentecostals, Baptists, and non-denominationalists to unite.

   c. Have you ever wondered how the one-world church of Revelation could come about given the doctrinal diversity of today's churches?
      1) All it takes is an experience powerful enough to cause people to set aside biblical distinctive.
      2) Remember that the Anti-Christ will come with signs and lying wonders.
         - He'll have some experiences for you that will shake you to the core.

- Jesus said that if it were possible, he would deceive the very elect.

    d. That mentality—and therefore the potential—already exist.

7. God's opinion of the of value experience as the determiner of truth is evident in the following situations:

    a. The Transfiguration - 2 Peter 1: 16-19
    Peter's experience on the mount was profound, but through Scripture, God gives an even more sure word of testimony.

    b. The Resurrection of Jesus - Luke 24
    On the road to Emmaus, Jesus didn't reveal himself to the two disciples until after He had affirmed their faith via Old Testament revelation. Scripture, not their personal experience with Christ, was to be the authoritative basis for their ministry.

    c. Personal Evangelism - Luke 16:31
    The rich man wanted to return from torment to warn his brothers, but Abraham said, "If they do not listen to Moses and the Prophets, neither will they be persuaded if someone rises from the dead." Scripture is sufficient for a powerful testimony—even more so than someone rising from the dead!

- **Mysticism**
1. Mysticism says that looking inside oneself is the key to finding truth, rather than looking to objective biblical revelation.

2. Mysticism, as it relates to deficient discernment, is elevating subjective feelings over biblical truth, or trying to determine truth through feelings.

3. We are to place our feelings under the authority of Scripture, not coddle or let them dictate our doctrinal positions.

    a. Jesus did not say, "Man shall not live by bread alone, but by *every feeling* that proceeds out of his heart." He said, "By *every word* that proceeds from the mouth of God."

    b. He did not say, "Go and make disciples of all the nations . . . teaching them to observe *all that they feel is true*." He said, "Teaching them to observe *all that I commanded you*."

    c. Paul didn't say, "Finally, brethren, whatever *seems* true, whatever *feels* honorable, whatever *feels* right, whatever *feels* pure, whatever *seems* lovely, etc., think on these things." He said, "Whatever *is* true, *is* honorable, *is* right, *is* pure, *is* lovely, etc."

4. Regarding the church, I've heard people say, "I love TBC. It just *feels right* being here."

    a. I appreciate their intent, and we certainly want everyone to feel welcome and at home.

I have nothing against feeling good. I like feeling good. It feels great to feel good!

b. But their words trouble me as much as someone who says, "I'm leaving TBC because it just *doesn't feel right* to me."

c. We aren't able to make such decisions on feelings, but on biblical guidelines:
   - Do we have a <u>high view of God</u>?
   - Do we have a <u>high view of Scripture</u>?
   - Do we teach <u>sound doctrine</u>?
   - Do we strive for <u>personal holiness</u>?
   - Do we operate under the <u>principle of spiritual authority</u>?
   - Do we <u>promote true worship and biblical fellowship</u>?

d. Those are the primary issues, yet if we're not discerning we can become distracted from those essentials and begin to base our decisions on lesser things.

5. You cannot be a mystic and a discerning person at the same time . . .

   - Because mysticism is *<u>grounded in personal, subjective feelings and intuition,</u>*

   - Whereas discernment is *<u>grounded in objective, biblical truth.</u>*

6. You cannot reason with a mystic because mysticism is unreasonable, whereas discernment reflects the reason and wisdom of God.

- **Avoiding Controversy**

1. Avoiding controversy can be good, but here I'm referring to the practice of avoiding controversy at the expense of sound doctrine.

2. This often involves sacrificing Christian convictions for the sake of establishing or maintaining personal relationships.

3. In our personal relationships, a common error is to believe that significant relationships (in or out of the church) must somehow exclude doctrinal convictions.

    a. Illustration:
    I've heard people say, "I never discuss religion or politics because they're too controversial and I'd rather not jeopardize my relationship with those who might disagree.

    b. Can you imagine Jesus saying, "I never discuss religion"? That's all He ever did discuss!

    c. When it comes to our Christian convictions, we are to confess Christ before men if we want Christ to confess us before the Father (Matt. 10:32)

    d. In addition to confessing Christ Himself, we are to speak the truth in love (Eph. 4:15).

e. We must be tactful and sensitive, but we must speak the truth when the situation requires our input.

   f. Not to do so may mean that we desire the approval of man more than God.

4. Within the church, another common way we attempt to avoid controversy is to tolerate sin rather than lovingly confronting it.

   a. We may fear that we may alienate folks if we confront them.

   b. We may fear that our motives might be misunderstood

   c. We may fear that will be labeled unloving, legalistic, or judgmental—and often we are labeled as such.

   d. Sometimes situations are extremely sensitive or potentially explosive due to the individuals or issues involved. And initially the price of confrontation may be high or the risk great. So the temptation may be strong simply to avoid conflict rather than dealing with it. But the rewards for following through are great also, because personal relationships and the overall health of the assembly are served.

5. God uses even serious factions for His purposes.

   a. It's true that ideally there should be no controversy or divisions in the church.

b. It's true that we have the Holy Spirit and should be unanimous in all things.

c. But it's also true that we must work to maintain the unity of the Spirit in the bond of peace.

d. It's also true that not every Christian is equally diligent in preserving that peace.

e. To assume that Christians will never disagree is to assume that Christians are perfect in holiness, wisdom, and motive. And that assumes too much this side of heaven.

f. 1 Cor. 11:18-19

- Until the Lord comes there will always be tares and disobedient Christians in churches, therefore there will always of necessity be factions.

- Factions (lit. *schismata*, from which we get our English word "schism") give faithful people an opportunity to prove their loyalty and spiritual maturity.

- I've seen that here. The depth of one's leadership and fidelity to the Lord and to this church is best seen at such times.

- **False Unity**

    1. I refer here to uniting with others at the expense of the gospel.

    2. See the principles of non-alignment in Appendix 4.

    3. Jesus prayed in John 17:33 that all believers would be perfected in unity so that the world may know that He was sent from the Father. In verse 17 of that chapter, He gave the guiding principle of true unity.

    4. Anything less than unity under biblical truth is less than true Christian unity.

    5. What we have now in major parts of the Christian community is a strong voice declaring that the gospel is the only legitimate point of unity. Everything else is of little value or divisive.

    6. When we set aside legitimate biblical distinctives in the name of Christian unity, we foster a false unity and:

        - Compromise our role as the pillar and support of the truth.

        - Imply that our points of agreement are more important than our points of disagreement, thereby relegating our points of disagreement to non-essentials.

- Imply that to accomplish anything of significance for Christ we must first surrender doctrinal precision.

- **Fear of Grieving the Holy Spirit**

A common accusation by those who are offering novel or extreme doctrines or experiences is that their critics are speaking against the Holy Spirit. That, of course, can be intimidating to some believers who sense that all is not right with what they're hearing, but are in fear of opposing what the Holy Spirit might be doing through these teachers.

But we are commanded to examine with great care all teachings or experiences purporting to be from God. That was the practice of the noble Bereans in Acts 17, and should be ours as well. I don't believe it's possible to be overly discerning in such matters.

SUMMARY:

I would love for the ministry to be a simple process of proclaiming the gospel and encouraging believers in their Christian walk. But from the outset Jesus said there will be false messiahs, wolves in sheep's clothing, and false teachers of every sort who prey upon the church. Additionally, many people will turn away from the truth, wanting to hear only what pleases them.

Through Paul God commanded church leaders to hold fast the faithful word which is in accordance with the teaching, that they may be able both to exhort in sound doctrine and to refute those contradict. There are many rebellious men, empty talkers and deceivers who must be silenced.

He called us to know His Word and apply it in our daily lives. He commands us to be diligent and not to fall prey to error or impurity. That requires discernment, so I conclude with a series of questions that each of us must consider prayerfully.

- What is my level of discernment?

- Am I impassioned about the things that matter to my Lord, or have I been distracted by the pull of the world?

- TARES IN THE CHURCH - Am I a Christian?

- IGNORANCE - Do I have an adequate and ever-increasing grasp of biblical principles which to make discerning decisions?

- SPIRITUAL PRIDE - Am I a humble learner, or am I too prideful to defer to those with greater knowledge and discernment?

- A SIMPLE FAITH - Do I try to hide my disinterest in things of the Lord behind a façade of "simple faith"?

- PERSONAL EXPERIENCE - Do I elevate personal religious experience over Scripture?

- MYSTICISM - Do I base my decisions on biblical principles or on subjective feelings and intuition?

- AVOIDING CONTROVERSY - Do I trust the Lord to honor His Word even when it leads to confrontation, or do I try to avoid controversy even when it means I have to violate God's Word?

- FALSE UNITY - Do I desire true biblical unity based on love and sound doctrine, or will I settle for something less?

- FEAR OF GRIEVING THE HOLY SPIRIT - Am I confident in my discernment, or am I intimidated by those who might accuse me of grieving the Holy Spirit?

Chapter 3 Homiletics

As a preacher plans his sermons, he must decide many things such as the needs of the audience, the Scriptures that can best provide the "medicine" for these needs, and what illustrations will make the needed message "stick." Certainly among these important decisions a preacher must make early in his preparation of a sermon is the *type* of sermon he will preach. Some, unfortunately, prepare the sermon and then "tack" a sermon label on it. Deciding on the type of sermon first provides the basis for the sermon's organizational structure, a very vital aspect of sermon preparation.

> *But hath in due times manifested his word through preaching, which is committed unto me according to the commandment of God our Saviour;*
> Titus 1:3

What Is Homiletics?

Homiletics is the art and science of preaching, communication. Communication is not talking, it is getting other people to listen and hear what you are saying. Five or ten minutes of listenable preaching are better than forty five minutes of boring preaching. Remember:

1. The Bible is alive so don't try to kill it. Do not bore people.
2. Know when to stop, sit down, and shut up. Avoid making the people happy twice.
3. Stay on the subject matter. Stay away from the rabbit trails unless the trail is sure to get the people to the place you are trying to take them.

What is Preaching?

Preaching is communicating divine truth to your people. It is the most important calling on earth. It is more important than being the President of the United States, more important than being on the Supreme Court or being a governor.

Preaching God's Word

It is more than imperative that the preacher remembers to preach by God's power and not with man's wisdom (1 Corinthians 2:4-5). Speak in the common man's language not with enticing words. The preacher must have the Holy Ghost's power upon him/her and be filled with the Spirit before one can begin to proclaim God's message.

Preachers are to give the Holy Ghost's message (1 Corinthians 2:3) realizing that Spirit filled preaching...
1. Sometimes brings success. (Ex. 3,000 saved at Pentecost)
2. Sometimes brings death. (Ex. Stephen & John the Baptist)
3. Sometimes exile or prison (Ex. John & Paul)

No matter what, leave the results up to God.

To Get a Message

Because all Scripture is given through inspiration of the Holy Spirit, sometimes it may require the preaching posing and answering the following questions before he/she can prepare the sermon.

1. Has the message come from God by my communion with the Holy Ghost?
   Communion is fellowship, communication, or social intercourse. Ask the Holy Spirit for a message. (2 Corinthians 13:14)

2. Have I prayed fervently and asked specifically for the sermon?
   (James 4:2)

3. Have I used common sense?
   What do the people need at this time?

4. What I have I learned that the people need to know?
   Share your personal Bible studying knowledge with your people. New and old ... review basics ... plus give new thoughts. (Matthew 13:52)

5. What can I preach to encourage the people to do right, affirming constantly the same truths?
   (Titus 3:8)

6. What can I give in the form of milk and meat?
   Do not choke the babies on meat. Do not starve the mature on milk all the time. (Hebrews 5:11-14; 1 Corinthians 3:2)

Selecting a Text

Here are five simple suggestions to guide you in selecting a text to preach from.

1. **Select a real text.** A Real Text is one which a complete statement, precept, or narrative used with the sense intended by the author. Single words or fragment texts are to be avoided. Any legitimate theme

can be based on a real text. Texts which are isolated from the context and accommodated to an application foreign to the purpose of the author are not proper texts. The words of Scripture cease to be Scripture when they are accommodated. "Let us do evil that good may come" is a sentence from the Bible, but when isolated from the context it is contrary to the teaching of the sacred author, and as such is not Scripture.

2. **Select the great doctrinal and ethical texts of the Bible.** Do not fear that these have been exhausted because they are frequently used. They are often used because they are great preaching texts. One need not fear, that he will be thought naïve or a beginner because he uses a familiar text; the great preachers of every age have used these great texts. The people are interested in them, because they have used them for comfort and light in dark places.

3. **Avoid texts which are known to be interpolations**, that is, portions which have crept into the later manuscripts through scribes' error or additions from marginal notes, which are not to be found in the oldest and most reliable manuscripts. These spurious* texts can be avoided by using the *Revised Version* for comparison in study. Let it be said that they are not numerous. However, the few which are found in the *Authorized Version* have often been used as texts. None of them contain false teaching, but many educated hearers know them, and a sermon based on a spurious text would have not authority with such persons.

4. **Avoid the sayings of uninspired men** when choosing a text. These sayings have their place in the Bible,

but they are not proper texts, because they lack divine authority. Many texts have been selected from the book of Job which is the words of Job's three friends. Some of these sound good when isolated, but all three of these speakers were in error and were rebuked by God. Others are Pharaoh, Satan, Balaam, Pilate, and any men whose words are reported, but who are not inspired apostles or prophets.

5. **Do not choose texts simply because they are odd or queer.** The serious minister has no time for novelties and curiosities. The preacher ought to be joyful, but not frivolous. Humor is not forbidden in the pulpit when it is in good taste, but one should not be funny at the expense of the Holy Word. Texts which seem queer appear so only because they are oriental or Old English idioms. A preacher once selected the text from Hosea, "Emphraim is a Cake not Turned," with the topic, "Half Baked." The only thing "half baked" in the modern sense of the term was that preacher's sermon.

Eight Rules of Interpretation

Before a text can be expressed in an intelligent theme and divided, it must be properly interpreted. Observe the following rules of interpretation.

1) **Interpret the text in the light of the context.** A verse of Scripture which seems to have one meaning may be seen to mean something else when the context is read. Examples include 1 Cor 2:9; Hebrews 12:1 and Colossians 2:21. Texts like these are so numerous that one is never safe in the interpretation of a text until the context has been studied.

2) **Interpret a text in harmony with the teaching of the whole Bible.** The Bible does not contradict itself, therefore when the text can have two meanings; the one is to be taken which is in harmony with the teaching of the body of Scripture.

3) **The text must be interpreted in harmony with sound, systematic doctrine.** Doctrines are formed after consulting the Bible's teaching on a subject. Therefore a single text which seems contrary must not be used against the well-established Bible doctrine. The orthodox tenets of the fundamental church have been subjected to two millenniums of scholarly interpretation. This does not guarantee their infallibility, but one should proceed with great fundamental consensus.

4) **A text should be taken literally** unless it is obviously figurative, or unless a literal interpretation would lead to absurdity or impossibility. The Bible was written in the common people's language and for average readers. Unrestricted spiritualizing and allegorizing do violence to the Bible and make it a little more than a playground for metaphysical minds. The spiritualizing done by Origen and a few other early fathers has had a bad influence on some later preachers, and some modern preachers. That spiritualizing is vain is seen by the fact that no two such interpreters get the same result. There are indeed some figures of speech in the Bible, but they are nearly every case where a Bible narrative is allegorized, the force application is inferior to the real and literal application.

5) **If possible, consult the original languages as help to interpretation.** But first a few lines of caution are needed. One should not try to make independent translations of words or passages of the Greek and Hebrew texts unless

one has studied the grammar of these languages. Some preachers with a doctrinal axe to grind quote Greek and Hebrew with a great show of authority when they have merely consulted a lexicon or an interlinear diglot. This is unsafe procedure, if not at times a dishonest one. There are preachers too, who quote the original words from hearsay, trusting the accuracy of another's research. The author has known of absurd renderings of Greek passages which he has traced through several persons all of whom quoted from hearsay. Furthermore, it is not good taste to quote Greek and Hebrew from the pulpit, for hardly anyone in the average congregation will appreciate the quotations. Give the people the benefits of thorough research, but do not display methods. Everyone knows that an artist uses a brush to paint his pictures, but they do not expect to see brush marked on the finished painting. These warnings need not discourage the Greek student; he can profit immeasurably by his studies. These are literally scores of passages the full depth of which cannot be seen in any English translation. There are also a vast number of homiletical hints which are discovered in the study of the original languages. Greek and Hebrew will greatly aid the minister to interpret his texts correctly, but let him keep these aids in his study where they belong.

6) **Make use of the scholar of other translators.** If the minister does not have a thorough knowledge of the original languages, he will be helped in interpreting the texts by comparing several literal and modern speech translations of the Bible.

7) **Furthermore, consult parallel passages.** Scripture is best interpreted by Scripture. If the same idea is expressed several places, but in somewhat different words, it is made clearer by comparison. If an ethical principle is

applied to somewhat different cases, it is seen to be general in application and not simply a local emergency measure. Some commands and prohibitions are of only local and temporary significance and others are meant for the whole church for all time. This problem of application can usually be solved by comparing parallel passages.

8) **Finally, consult one of some good commentaries of the critical, exegetical type.** Devotional commentaries seldom give much attention to interpretation, although they are helpful in suggesting points for elaboration, but here we are interested only in the interpretation of the text which must come before elaboration. The writers of the good exegetical commentaries were careful Biblical scholars conversant with theology and the original languages, and while they are not infallible, of course, their opinions are worth considering along with one's own in the process of interpreting the text. Do not be slavish follower of commentaries, but does not reject their explanations without good reason and careful study either.

Types of Sermons

There are six types of sermons that are prevalent in today's Church:

   A. Sermons based on a word
   Take one word. Study it out. Preach and teach everything you have learned about it. For example, you could preach a message about love, charity—(1 Corinthians 13), deliverance, patience, compassion, sanctification, etc.

B. Sermons based on topics
   Pick a topic such as:
   1. How to have a happy marriage – family
   2. What do we owe the government? Respect, taxes, involvement, prayer.
   3. How to have revival
   4. Successful soul-winning
   5. Getting things through prayer
   6. How to love God
         Etc....

C. Sermons based on doctrine
   1. Soteriology – salvation
   2. Theology proper – God
   3. Pneumatology – Holy Spirit
   4. Christology – Jesus Christ
   5. Eschatology – end time events
   6. Bibiology – the Bible
   7. Angelology – Angels, Satan, demons
   8. Anthropology – man
   9. The Virgin Birth – Immaculate conception
   10. The Blood Atonement
   11. Bodily Resurrection
         Etc....

D. Sermons based on characters
   1. Eli, the father who did not restrain his kids.
   2. Reuben, the unstable father.
   3. Lot, the backslidden father.
   4. Peter, James, etc....
   5. Every man, every woman, major and minor in the Bible can be preached on.

E. Sermons based on the books of the Bible
Preach through any one of the 66 books in the Bible (verse-by-verse; chapter-by-chapter; or thought-by-thought).

F. Sermons based on occasions
   1. Wedding, funerals
   2. New years
   3. Valentine's day (marriage)
   4. Presidents day (government – Romans 13)
   5. Easter – Resurrection Day
   6. Memorial day (remember)
   7. Children's, Father's, Mother's, or Grandparent's Day
   8. Independence day (dependence)
   9. Labor day (work ethic)
   10. Columbus day (God's leadership)
   11. Thanksgiving day (Horrible sin of ingratitude)
   12. Christmas day (Virgin birth)
       Etc....

Types of Preaching

Just as there are six types of sermons, there are also six different types of preaching. (2 Timothy 4:2)

A. Reproof – to refute, expose false teaching and practice
(Job 26:11; Proverbs 1:23; Proverbs 1:25; Proverbs 1:30; Proverbs 5:12; Proverbs 10:17; Proverbs 12:1; Proverbs 13:18; Proverbs 15:5; Proverbs 15:10; Proverbs 15:31-32; Proverbs 17:10; Proverbs 29:15; 2 Timothy 3:16)

B. Rebuke – to scold in love
(Proverbs 9:8; Proverbs 13:1; Proverbs 13:8; Proverbs 24:25; Proverbs 27:5; Ecclesiastes 7:5; Luke 17:3; 1 Timothy 5:20; 2 Timothy 4:2; Titus 1:13; Titus 2:15)

C. Exhort
    a. Interpreted "advocate" – "to run to one's side and pick him up"
(1 John 2:1)

    b. Help, encourage, assurance and comfort sermons
(1 Thessalonians 4:1; 1 Thessalonians 5:14; 1 Timothy 6:2; 2 Timothy 4:2; Titus 1:9; Titus 2:6; Titus 2:9; Titus 2:15; Hebrews 3:13; 1 Peter 5:1)

D. Devotional
  1. Deals with our intimate relationship to God.

  2. Worship, communion with the Holy Ghost, seeking the Lord, hearing His voice, etc.

E. Exegetical
Explanation or interpretation of the Bible.

F. Expository
Expose everything a portion of Scripture says.

The Sermon
Each sermon is in three parts:
- The Introduction
- Body of the message
- The Conclusion / Invitation

- Another way to say it...
    - Tell them what you are going to say
    - Then say it
    - Then tell them what you have said

A. The Introduction
The Introduction should...
- Be an accurate signpost pointing to the sermon.
- Create a hunger for the rest of the message.
- Be a creation of intrigue.
- Lead the people to feel that the sermon has the answer to an individual need.
- Get people desirous for the preacher to continue.
- Be the most articulate part of the sermon.

The Introduction could...
- Be a question that needs an answer
- Be a statement that needs a completion
- Create curiosity as to where the speaker is going.

The title of the sermon should not be more spectacular than the sermon. Jesus got right to the point. Some preachers can build to a climax and have people hang on long enough to get the one point – MOST CANNOT! So let the cat out of the bag at the beginning so they know what you are talking about right from the start. We are preachers not story tellers. **Do not try to be a great preacher, be a clear preacher.** Our words should not be a mystery but **crystal clear**. (1 Corinthians 14:8-9)

Some preachers read a text, do not give a title, chase rabbits, say some good things, ramble on, close and then leave hearers puzzled. The people wonder, "What was that all about?" We should go to the other extreme. We should speak in such clear and simple tones that it is not only perfectly understood what we said, but it is **impossible to misunderstand what we said.** (2 Corinthians 3:12)

The following four points should help achieve this in the introduction:
1. Read the scriptures **clearly**. Make sure the scriptures fit your message exactly.
2. Say a short public prayer asking God to help the **hearers to understand your specific subject.** You might want to bring up the subject in your prayer.
3. **Repeat** the title of your message **loudly and clearly** at least two to four times during your introduction.
4. Have a well thought out brief introduction of the subject. Do not waste time in the pulpit. Again, clarity is the goal (1 Corinthians 14:10-12). **Build up the church, do not confuse the church!**

B. The Body of the Sermon

The first aspect of the body of your sermon is to come up with a skeleton outline regarding the text and subject the Holy Spirit has led you to preach on.

- Examples of skeleton outlines could include:
  1. Pointed message
     Some truths we must preach require many points depending on the subject. Certainly these subjects would need more than one point:
     - How to have a happy family

- How to handle your finances
- How to go soul winning
- How to interpret scripture
- Steps of man's degeneracy (Romans 1)
- Possibilities of faith---etc.

2. One Great Truth

    Preach a whole sermon stressing just one great truth:
    - Duty
    - Compassion
    - Others
    - Commitment

3. Alliteration

    Repetitions of the same first letter or sound in a group of words:
    - Titus 2:14---Salvation, Sanctification, Service
    - Philemon's love---Refreshing, Receiving, Reciprocating
    - Spirit filled Attitudes---Ephesians 5:18-21---Singing, Sanctification, Submission

4. Acrostic

    Word formed from the first letters of other words.
    - Forsaking All I Trust Him
    - God's Riches At Christ's Expense
    - God's Resources At Christian Experiences

5. Verses that outline themselves
   Look up in your Bible and notice how easily these verses outline themselves:

- James 3:17
- Titus 2:4-5
- 1 Corinthians 13:4-8
- 2 Chronicles 7:14

- The second aspect now of your sermon is to add some meat to the skeleton outline. You can fill in the body of the sermon by using:
  1. Definition of terms
     Use dictionary or concordance and then explain terms to the people. Do not presume they know what words mean. (Nehemiah 8:8)

  2. Illustrations
     a. Personal illustrations
     b. Borrowed illustrations from books
     c. People in the Bible that might illustrate the point.
     d. Facts pertaining to the topic from history, science, archaeology, encyclopedia, etc.
     e. Stories that make a point.

  3. Poems—Hymns
     For example, an appropriate poem or hymn that exactly fits the point.

  4. Practical aspects
     Do not let people figure it out, explain it to them. For instance, explain what a "prayer closet" is.

C. The Conclusion
   Remember: Tell them what you are going to say (the introduction), then say it (the body) and then tell them what you said (the conclusion). Take this opportunity to one more time ex-

plain the message. It would be wise to at least read your points out loud again.

Also if you feel that something was not clear in the message; try to clear it up briefly. Do not bore people by preaching your whole sermon again, just highlight your main points! This will refresh their memory of something you may have said thirty minutes ago.

D. The Invitation

The invitation is not the time to put our Bibles away, straighten up the Hymnals, clean up the pews, and get our coats and hats. It is the time to respond to God. The preacher should make that clear. It is the time to apply the truth to our lives. The goal is not to get people to the altar, but to have people take the message into their lives and be doers of God's word and not hearers only.

We should try to get God's people to pray about the application of the message. An altar call is an appropriate way to do this. Invite them to come and pray. The congregation could sing an appropriate hymn.

An appeal for the lost to be saved should also be given. They may come forward or may not. If they come forward pair them off with a soul winner. If they do not come forward then just pray for them and with them for salvation. You could perhaps repeat a sinner's prayer of repentance slowly for them to say from their heart to God. Remember, "woe is unto, if I preach not the gospel!" (1 Corinthians 9:16)

Chapter 4 What Is Expository Preaching

Biblical preaching's authenticity is significantly tarnished by contemporary communicator's being more concerned with personal relevance than God's revelation. Scripture unmistakably requires a proclamation focused on God's will and mankind's obligation to obey. With men wholly committed to God's Word, the expository method commends itself as preaching that is true to the Bible. The method presupposes an exegetical process to extract the God-intended meaning of Scripture and an explanation of that meaning in a contemporary understandable way. The biblical essence and apostolic spirit of expository preaching need to be recaptured in the training of men new committed to "preaching the Word."

Discussions about preaching divide it into three types: topical, textual, and expositional. Topical messages usually combine a series of Bible verses that loosely connect with a theme. Textual preaching use a short text or passage that generally serves as a gateway into whatever subject the preacher chooses to address. Neither the topical nor the textual method represents a serious effort to interpret, understand, explain, or apply God's truth in the context of the Scripture(s) used.

By contrast, expositional preaching focuses predominantly on the text(s) under consideration along with its (their) context(s). Exposition normally concentrates on a single text of Scripture, but it is sometimes possible for a thematic/theological message or a historical/biographical discourse to be expositional in nature. An exposition may treat any length of passage.

One way to clarify expository preaching is to identify what it is not.

1. It is not a commentary running from word to word and verse to verse without unity, outline, and pervasive drive.
2. It is not rambling comments and offhand remarks about a passage without a background of thorough exegesis and logical order.

3. It is not a mass of disconnected suggestions and interferences based on the surface meaning of a passage, but not sustained by a depth-and-breadth study of the text.
4. It is not pure exegesis, no matter how scholarly, if it lacks a theme, thesis, outline and development.
5. It is not a mere structural outline of a passage with a few supporting comments, but without other rhetorical and sermonic elements.
6. It is not a topical homily using scattered parts of the passage, but omitting discussion of other equally important parts.
7. It is not a chopped-up collection of grammatical findings and quotations from commentaries without a fusing of the same into smooth, flowing, interesting, and compelling message.
8. It is not a Sunday School-lesson type of discussion that has an outline of the contents, informality, and fervency, but lacks sermonic structure and rhetorical ingredients.
9. It is not a Bible reading that links a number of scattered passages treating a common theme, but fails to handle any of them in a thorough, grammatical, and contextual manner.
10. It is not the ordinary devotional or prayer meeting talk that combines running commentary, rambling remarks, disconnected suggestions, and personal reactions into a semi-inspirational discussion, but lacks the benefit of the basic exegetical-contextual study and persuasive elements.

Defining Expository Preaching

Before proceeding further, consider the English word group; "expose, exposition, expositor, expository." According to Webster, an exposition is a discourse to convey information or explain what is difficult to understand. Application of this to preaching requires that an expositor be one who explains Scripture by laying open the text to public view in order to set forth its meaning, explain what is difficult to understand, and make appropriate application.

John Calvin's centuries-old understanding of exposition:

> First of all, Calvin understood preaching to be the explication of Scripture. The words of Scripture are the source and content of preaching. As an expositor, Calvin brought to the

task of preaching all the skills of a humanist scholar. As an interpreter, Calvin explicated the text, seeking its natural, it's true, it's scriptural meaning . . . Preaching is not only the explication of Scripture; it is also the application of Scripture. Just as Calvin explicated Scripture word by word, so he applied the Scripture sentence by sentence to the life and experience of his congregation.

Definitions of expository preaching often lean toward either the preparation or the organizational aspects of the process without delineating between content and form. Andrew Blackwood leaned toward the technical aspect when he wrote, "Expository preaching means that the light for any sermon comes mainly from a Bible passage larger than two or three consecutive verses. John Scott leans toward the hermeneutical aspect when he says, "Properly speaking 'exposition' has a much broader meaning. It refers to the content of the sermon (biblical truth) rather than its style (a running commentary)." Others would, of course, object to his equating expository style with a running commentary.

The classic three-point sermon, a didactic type of preaching often hears from many of these pulpits, which had its origins in the nineteenth century, abandons the biblical world and its literary forms. George Swank suggests that the linear, didactic expository method seems more from a cultural than biblical impetus. "The sermon based on neat, orderly, deductive logic, which is the kind of preaching that most of us have expected to hear, is derived from an age of writing.

J. Alfred Smith implies that black preachers have made the distinction between the diversity of definition from two very different homiletical endeavors, both of which have indiscriminately been called expository preaching. Smith ascertains that the black preacher makes the distinction while practicing a cultural style of narrative preaching which little resemblance to the linear, didactic style has often termed expository. "Early black preachers, who took seriously the preaching responsibility, worked tirelessly to perfect the preaching gift of storytelling. Their sermons were artistic pieces of style related to sound principles of hermeneutics.

The definition that I will use is a style or method of preaching God's Word that seeks to logically expose the biblical text to the mind and will of the people of God. The preacher is to passionately open up, uncover, and lay bare the rich truths contained in Holy Writ and he is to urge the people of God to understand and obey the truth that they have just learned, doing all this to the glory of Jesus Christ.

Similarly, Jerry Vines and Jim Shaddix define expository preaching as "the process of lying open a biblical text in such a way that its original meaning is brought to bear on the lives of contemporary listeners." Ramesh Richards describes this way of preaching when he states, "Expository preaching is the contemporization of the central proposition of a biblical text that is derived from proper methods of interpretation and declared through effective means of communication to inform minds, instruct hearts, and influence behavior toward godliness."

A separate definition to assist us in our quest for what exposition is, namely, "At its best, expository preaching is the presentation of biblical truth, derived from and transmitted through historical, grammatical, Spirit-guided study of a passage in its context, which the Holy Spirit applies first to the life of the preacher and then through him to his congregation.

More simply put, expository preaching is proclaiming God's Word, verse by verse. This acquaints the typical evangelical who is not familiar with the word "expository." Likewise, many people in today's churches will understand this rare breed of sermon when they informed that the Pastor is "preaching through a book" of the Bible.

One could also communicate the truth of this method of proclamation by virtually identifying what exposition is not. This kind of preaching is not topical, that is, it is not built upon or around a theological or biographical subject matter. At one extreme, it is not a series of cross references assembled with exegesis, and on the other extreme, it is not a grouping a scholarly, exegetical data that has no them or homiletically rhetoric. Dr. Richard Mayhue describes it "It is not a chopped-up collection of grammatical findings and quotations from commentaries without a fusing of the same into a smooth, flowing, interesting, and compelling message." Lastly, it is not a rambling discus-discussion about the Bible rather preaching the Bible.

"What saith the Lord" is the beginning and ending of expository preaching. It begins in the Bible and ends in the Bible and all that intervenes springs from the Bible. In other words, expository preaching is Bible-centered preaching. In summary, expository preaching is a sermon from a man, who above all else, wants to glorify His Lord by studying a passage to find out what it means to God (so many wrongly think that the object of the preposition during study is "me"), and then he persuasively proclaims that truth, in context, interpreted in a grammatical, historical way, revolving around a central proposition, to a group of His sheep.

Expository preaching, both in content and organization, remains the best method for the communicator to the western mindset, the average American audience today. It is still the best way to assure one that he is conveying the biblical revelation of God and His will because the preacher is "confined to biblical truth." It would be a tragedy for the Western church to lose that close connection with Scripture in preaching.

At the same time there are some great values in seeking to make a distinction between expository content and expository organization. It would also be a great tragedy if, in swearing allegiance to a particular preaching style, the communicator hindered understanding of the very content he desires to share. That tragedy becomes a real possibility when the communication of the gospel to other cultures within a framework of western thinking is attempted. It is even a possibility within a western culture when a potential audience has been heavily influenced by post-modern thought.

The very nature of the message entrusted to the communicator by God requires him to consider the form as well as the content of preaching. Accepting a view which makes a distinction between expository content and organization enables the preacher to maintain fidelity to Scripture by means of a historical-grammatical hermeneutic, while adapting to an audience in the way those biblical truths are communicated. In this way narrative preaching, dialogue preaching, debate, drama, storytelling, and inductive preaching can serve as viable communicative styles while at the same time the preacher faithfully exposits the God-given meaning of any text. The expository method of preparing content is demanded by Scripture and should not be abandoned. The method of organization commonly called expository preaching is not demanded by Scripture and therefore only one of many styles of preaching available to the preacher today.

In summary, the following minimal elements identify expository preaching:

1. The message finds its sole source in Scripture.
2. The message is extracted from Scripture through careful exegesis.
3. The message preparation correctly interprets Scripture in its normal sense and its context.
4. The message clearly explains the original God-intended meaning of Scripture.
5. The message applies the Scriptural meaning for today.

Examine Greer Boyce's definition of expository preaching:

> In short, expository preaching demands that, by careful analysis of each text within its immediate context and the setting of the book to which it belong, the full power of modern exegetical and theological scholarship is brought to bear upon our treatment of the Bible. The objective is not that the preacher may parade all this scholarship in the pulpit. Rather, it is that the preacher may speak faithfully out of solid knowledge of his text, and mount the pulpit steps as, at least, "a workman who has no need to be ashamed, rightly handling the word of truth."
>
> The preacher's final step is the most crucial and most perilous of all. It is to relate the biblical message both faithfully and relevantly to modern life. At this point all his skill as a craftsman must come into play. We must be warned that faithful exposition of a text does not of itself produce an effective

sermon. We need also be warned, however, that faithfulness to the text is not to be sacrificed for the sake of what we presume to be relevancy. This sacrifice too many modern preachers seem willing to make, producing, as a result, sermons that are a compound of moralistic advice, their own unauthoritative and sometimes unwise opinions, and the latest psychology. Expository preaching, by insisting that the message of the sermon coincide with the theme of the text, calls the preacher back to his true task: the proclamation of the Word of God in and through the Bible.

Preaching with Authority: Three Characteristics of Expository Preaching

Authentic expository preaching is marked by three distinct characteristics: authority, reverence, and centrality. Expository preaching is authoritative because it stands upon the very authority of the Bible as the word of God. Such preaching requires and reinforces a sense of reverent expectation on the part of God's people. Finally, expository preaching demands the central place in Christian worship and is respected as the event through which the living God speaks to his people.

A keen analysis of our contemporary age comes from the sociologist Richard Sennett of New York University. Sennett notes that in times past a major anxiety of most persons was loss of governing authority. Now, the tables have been turned, and modern persons are anxious about any authority over them: "We have come to fear the influence of authority as a threat to our liberties, in the family and in society at large." If previous generations feared the absence of authority, today we see "a fear of authority when it exists."

Some homileticians suggest that preachers should simply embrace this new worldview and surrender any claim to an authoritative message. Those who have lost confidence in the authority of the Bible as the word of God are left with little to say and no authority for their message. Fred Craddock, among the most influential figures in recent homiletic thought, famously describes today's preacher "as one without authority." His portrait of the preacher's predicament is haunting: "The old thunderbolts rust in the attic while the minister tries to lead his people through the morass of relativities and proximate possibilities." "No longer can the preacher presuppose the general recognition of his authority as a clergyman, or the authority of his institution, or the authority of Scripture," Craddock argues. Summarizing the predicament of the postmodern preacher, he relates that the preacher "seriously asks himself whether he should continue to serve up monologue in a dialogical world."

The obvious question to pose to Craddock's analysis is this: If we have no authoritative message, why preach? Without authority, the preacher and the congregation are involved in a massive waste of precious time. The very idea that preaching can be transformed into a dialogue between the pulpit and the pew indicates the confusion of our era.

Contrasted to this is the note of authority found in all true expository preaching. Martyn Lloyd-Jones notes:

> *Any study of church history, and particularly any study of the great periods of revival or reawakening, demonstrates above everything else just this one fact: that the Christian Church during all such periods has spoken with authority. The great characteristic of all revivals has been the authority of the preacher. There seemed to be something new, extra, and irresistible in what he declared on behalf of God.*

The preacher dares to speak on behalf of God. He stands in the pulpit as a steward "of the mysteries of God" (1 Cor. 4:1) and declares the truth of God's word, proclaims the power of that word, and applies the word to life. This is admittedly an audacious act. No one should even contemplate such an endeavor without absolute confidence in a divine call to preach and in the unblemished authority of the Scriptures.

In the final analysis, the ultimate authority for preaching is the authority of the Bible as the word of God. Without this authority, the preacher stands naked and silent before the congregation and the watching world. If the Bible is not the word of God, the preacher is involved in an act of self-delusion or professional pretension.

Standing on the authority of Scripture, the preacher declares a truth received, not a message invented. The teaching office is not an advisory role based on religious expertise, but a prophetic function whereby God speaks to his people.

Authentic expository preaching is also marked by reverence. The congregation that gathered before Ezra and the other preachers demonstrated a love and reverence for the word of God (Neh. 8). When the book was read, the people stood up. This act of standing reveals the heart of the people and their sense of expectation as the word was read and preached.

Expository preaching requires an attitude of reverence on the part of the congregation. Preaching is not a dialogue, but it does involve at least two parties—the preacher and the congregation. The congregation's role in the preaching event is to hear, receive, and obey the word of God. In so doing, the church demonstrates reverence for the preaching and teaching of the Bible and understands that the sermon brings the word of Christ near to the congregation. This is true worship.

Lacking reverence for the word of God, many congregations are caught in a frantic quest for significance in worship. Christians leave worship services asking each other, "Did you get anything out of that?" Churches produce surveys to measure expectations for worship: Would you like more music? What kind? How about drama? Is our preacher sufficiently creative?

Expository preaching demands a very different set of questions. Will I obey the word of God? How must my thinking be realigned by Scripture? How must I change my behavior to be fully obedient to the word? These questions reveal submission to the authority of God and reverence for the Bible as his word.

Likewise, the preacher must demonstrate his own reverence for God's word by dealing truthfully and responsibly with the text. He must not be flippant or casual, much less dismissive or disrespectful. Of this we can be certain; no congregation will revere the Bible more than the preacher does.

If expository preaching is authoritative, and if it demands reverence, it must also be at the center of Christian worship. Worship properly directed to the honor and glory of God will find its center in the reading and preaching of the word of God. Expository preaching cannot be assigned a supporting role in the act of worship—it must be central.

In the course of the Reformation, Luther's driving purpose was to restore preaching to its proper place in Christian worship. Referring to the incident between Mary and Martha in Luke 10, Luther reminded his congregation and students that Jesus Christ declared that "only one thing is necessary," the preaching of the word (Luke 10:42). Therefore, Luther's central concern was to reform worship in the churches by re-establishing there the centrality of the reading and preaching of the word.

That same reformation is needed in American evangelicalism today. Expository preaching must once again be central to the life of the church and central to Christian worship. In the end, the church will not be judged by its Lord for the quality of its music but for the faithfulness of its preaching.

When today's evangelicals speak casually of the distinction between worship and preaching (meaning that the church will enjoy an offering of music before adding on a bit of preaching), they betray their misunderstanding of both worship and the act of preaching. Worship is not something we do before we settle down for the word of God; it is the act through which the people of God direct all their attentiveness to the one true and living God who speaks to them and receives their praises. God is most beautifully praised when his people hear his word, love his word, and obey his word.

As in the Reformation, the most important corrective to our corruption of worship (and defense against the consumerist demands of that day) is to rightly return expository preaching and the public reading of God's word to primacy and centrality in worship. Only then will the "missing jewel" be truly rediscovered.

Exposition Must Have Application[1]
There is scarcely anything as dull and meaningless as Bible doctrine taught for its own sake. Truth divorced from life is not truth in its Biblical sense, but something else and something less. Theology is a set of facts concerning God, man and the world. These facts may be, and often are, set forth as values in themselves; and there lies the snare both for the teacher and for the hearer.

The Bible is among other things a book of revealed truth. That is, certain facts are revealed that could not be discovered by the most brilliant mind. These facts are of such a nature as to be past finding out. They were hidden behind a veil, and until certain men who spoke as they were moved by the Holy Ghost took away that veil, no mortal man could know them. This lifting of the veil of unknowing from undiscoverable things we call divine revelation.

The Bible, however, is more than a volume of hitherto unknown facts about God, man and the universe. It is a book of exhortation based upon those facts. By far the greater portion of the book is devoted to an urgent effort to persuade people to alter their ways and bring their lives into harmony with the will of God as set forth in its pages.

No man is better for knowing that God in the beginning created the havens and the earth. The devil knows that, and so did Ahab and

---
[1] A. W. Tozer *Of God and Men* (Harrisburg, Penn: Christian Publications, 1960) Ch. 7

Judas Iscariot. No man is better for knowing that God so loved the world of men that he gave his only begotten Son to die for their redemption. In hell there are millions that know that. Theological truth is useless until it is obeyed.

What is generally overlooked is that truth as set forth in the Christian Scriptures is a moral thing; it is not addressed to the intellect only, but to the will also. It addresses itself to the total man, and its obligations cannot be discharged by grasping it mentally. Truth engages the citadel of the human heart and is not satisfied until it has conquered everything there. The will must come forth and surrender its sword. It must stand at attention to receive orders, and those orders it must joyfully obey. Short of this any knowledge of Christian truth is inadequate and unavailing.

Bible exposition without moral application raises no opposition. Is only when the hearer is made to understand that truth is in conflict with his heart that resistance sets in? As long as people can hear orthodox truth divorced from life they will attend and support churches and institutions without objection. The truth is a lovely song, become sweet by long and tender association; and since it asks nothing but a few dollars, and offers good music, pleasant friendships and a comfortable sense of wellbeing, it meets with no resistance from the faithful. Much that passes for New Testament Christianity is little more than objective truth sweetened with song and made palatable by religious entertainment.

Probably no other portion of the Scriptures can compare with the Pauline Epistles when it comes to making artificial saints. Peter warned that the unlearned and unstable would wrest Paul's writings to their own destruction, and we have only to visit the average Bible Conference and listen to a few lectures to know what he meant. The ominous thing is that the Pauline doctrines may be taught with complete faithfulness to the letter of the text without making the hearers one whit better. The teacher may, and often does, so teach the truth as to leave the hearers without a sense of moral obligation.

One reason for the divorce between truth and life may be the lack of the Spirit's illumination. Another surely is the teacher's unwillingness to get into trouble. Any many with fair pulpit gifts can get on with the average congregation if he just "feeds" them and lets them alone. Give them plenty of objective truth and never hint that they are wrong and should be set right, and they will be content.

On the other hand, the man who preaches truth and applies it to the lives of his hearers will feel the nails and the thorns. He will lead a hard life, but a glorious one. May God rise up many such prophets. The church needs them badly.

Chapter 5 The Need for Expository Preaching

Puritan theologian William Perkins wrote that preaching "has four great principles: to read the text distinctly, from canonical Scripture; to give it sense and understanding according to the Scripture itself; to collect a few profitable points of doctrine out of its natural sense; and to apply, if you have the gift, the doctrines to the life and manner of men in a simple and plain speech.

There is something refreshingly simply about that description. Our aim as preachers is not to be the most erudite scholar of the age. Our aim is not titillate and amuse. Our aim is not to build a big church.

Our aim is to take the sacred text, explain what it means, tie it to other scriptures so people can see the whole a little better, and apply it to life so it bites and heals, instructs, and edifies. What better way to accomplish this end than expository preaching?

Practical Justifications for Expository Preaching

The Bible gives us both the models of exposition and the mandates for it. Let's examine some models first. Nehemiah 8:8 gives the tendency or flavor for expository preaching. This was more than just reading or even translating. It contained study, explanation, and exhortation.

From the teacher's perspective, Ezra did more than simply recite the biblical text, Ezra 7:10 says that he set his heart to study the law of the LORD, and to practice it and to teach His statutes and ordinances in Israel. This implies the painstaking efforts undertaken by Ezra to properly teach all that the Lord had commanded (after thorough study).

In terms of a pattern that has great influence, Paul told the Ephesians that had discharged all his duty in Acts 20:26-27. Anything less than teaching the entire corpus would have been unacceptable to the Lord, and to Paul. Surely, the only way to accomplish this task in three years was systematically and expositionally (ex. Book by book).

Dr. Mayhue gives some examples of exposition when he states, "A particular example is Jesus' expounding on Isa 61:1-2 in the synagogue (Luke 4:16-22). He later gave a thematic exposition of Himself to the disciples on the road to Emmaus (Luke 24: 27, 32, 44-47). Phillip in Acts 8:27-35 expounded Isa 53:7-8 for the Ethiopian eunuch. Stephan preached a historical/biographical expository sermon to the Jews before they stoned him (Acts 7:2-53).

This model is also followed by a mandate or directive by the Spirit of God Himself. The Holy Spirit, using the human agent Paul, said in 2 Tim 4:1-2, "I solemnly charge you in the presence of God and of Christ Jesus, who is to judge the living and the dead, and by His appearing and His kingdom: preach the word; be ready in season and out of season; reprove, rebuke, exhort, with great patience and instruction." This command from God to herald the Word must be taken to proclaim all of God's Word, and the most obvious way to do that is just the way it was breathed out, that is, one verse at a time, one after another.

Theologically, since all Scripture is inspired, sufficient, and contains the mind of the Lord, then it is our duty to teach and to preach all of it in its entirety. It saves and sanctifies, so we must, as Paul says in 2 Tim 2:15-16, study. Only responsible workmen need apply for expository preaching.

This idea can be summed up by the International Council on Biblical Inerrancy, which states, "WE AFFIRM that the only type of preaching which sufficiently conveys the divine revelation and its proper application to life is that which faithfully expounds the text of Scripture as the Word of God. WE DENY that the preacher has any message apart from the text of Scripture."

Lastly, it is an elder duty to know doctrine so well that "he may be able both to exhort in sound doctrine and to refute those who contradict" (Tit. 1:9). This can only be done after careful exegetical study of all of the God's Words. In order to teach and warn, the leg work of systematic study must be accomplished. Expository preaching is a great way to train up elders to teach every truth and warn of every error.

There are a variety of practical validations for expository preaching. The most important is that preaching the whole counsel of God edifies both the Pastor and his congregation. Spurgeon, even though he was not an expository preacher, had a lot of insight in this area, saying, "No truth is to be kept back ... It is not true that some doctrines are only for the initiated; there is nothing in the Bible which is ashamed of the light. ... Cautious reticence is, in nine cases out of ten, cowardly betrayal. The best policy is never to be politic, but to proclaim every atom of the truth so far as God has taught it to you... All revealed truth in harmonious proportion must be yours." Verse by verse teaching provides the congregation God's entire revealed mind, from His love to His wrath, from divine sovereignty to human responsibility, and form doctrine to duty. Every subject is covered, it is handled in proper proportions, and it is all covered exactly as God revealed it. Both the pastor and his flock become well rounded theologically, as they are forced to study the entire body of God's Word. This breadth of biblical knowledge is irreplaceable. The very core of exposition is the deep diving into the text and extracting out more the precious one of God's Word. This should give the layman more than he could get with just his/her English text.

Additionally, biblical explication inhibits the potential of the shepherd riding his favorite hobby horses. This particular, problem saddle can be mounted too often by topical preaching. Expository preaching prevents this, and on the flip side, it forces the preacher to deal with every problem text or controversial subject. The afflicted are comforted and the comforted are afflicted. Paul told Timothy to preach in such a variegated manner, saying, "reprove, rebuke, exhort" (2 Tim 4:2). Verse by verse preaching will cover each of these commanded modes.

This manner of preaching also actually serves as a self-protection device in the pastorate which, by nature, is laden with potential pitfalls. The pastor must preach the next set of verses and a well-trained congregation will be able to right through an under prepared or doctrinally compromised view, since they are also seeing the context, etc. This safety measure does exactly what Ramesh Richard says, "Basically, expository preaching helps the preacher promote God's agenda for his people." God's Word, through expository preaching, stays in the forefront, which is its rightly deserved place of honor.

Expository sermons are very practical because they save both time and stress. Every pastor knows the pressure of having to 'pick' a passage that is simultaneously educational, motivational, Spirit directed, and encouraged. This pressure is horrendous and it can be totally avoided by letting the Lord direct you and the congregation by heralding the next set of verses. How great it is to arrive at the study on Tuesday morning and know exactly what the Lord wants you to preach, namely, the next sea of verses! Still on the pragmatic vein, I always suggest to vacationers and other travelers that they need to only ask a potential church one question to ascertain if it will exalt Jesus Christ during Sunday morning worship: "if your Pastor is preaching a book of the Bible verse by verse, which book is he preaching?" Most liberal churches run from expository preaching and much can be learned from any Protestant church that exposes people to a central truth in a set of verses.

Lastly, one more practical justification is in order, and that is expository preaching helps the Pastor stay ahead of an ever increasing and mature flock. No matter how godly and scripturally insightful they are, they cannot devote 15-30 hours per week studying the text and therefore the most godly and educated can still worship and learn much in this type of proclamation from the pulpit.

Considering Expositional Advantages
Expository preaching best emulates biblical preaching both in content and style. This is the chief benefit. Besides this, other advantages listed in random order include the following:
11. Expositional preaching best achieves the biblical intent of preaching: delivering God's message.

12. Expositional preaching promotes scripturally authoritative preaching.
13. Expositional preaching magnifies God's Word.
14. Expositional preaching provides a storehouse of preaching materials.
15. Expositional preaching develops the pastor as a man of God's Word.
16. Expositional preaching ensures the highest level of Bible knowledge for the flock.
17. Expositional preaching promotes thinking and living biblically.
18. Expositional preaching encourages both depth and comprehensiveness.
19. Expositional preaching forces the treatment of hard-to-interpret texts.
20. Expositional preaching allows for handling broad theological themes.
21. Expositional preaching keeps preachers away from ruts and hobby horses.
22. Expositional preaching prevents the insertion of human ideas.
23. Expositional preaching guards against misinterpretation of the biblical text.
24. Expositional preaching imitates the preaching Christ and the apostles.
25. Expositional preaching brings out the best in the expositor.

8 Advantages of Heart-changing, Expository Preaching[2]

Expository preaching:

1. Does justice to the biblical material which makes it clear that God works through his word to change people's lives—as it 'uncages the lion' and allows God's word to speak.
2. Acknowledges that is God alone, through the Spirit, who works in people's lives, and that it is not our job to change people through clever or inspiring communication.
3. Minimizes the danger of manipulating people, because the text itself controls what we say and how we say it. The Bible

---

[2] Gary Millar and Phil Campbell, *Saving Eutychus: How to Preach God's Word and Keep People Awake* (Kingsford NSW, Australia: Matthias Media, 2013), 40-41.

leaves little room for us to return repeatedly to our current bugbears and hobbyhorses.
4. Minimizes the danger of abusing power, because a sermon driven by the text creates an instant safeguard against using the Bible to bludgeon (or caress) people into doing or thinking what we want them to do or think.
5. Removes the need to rely on our personality. While we all feed the weight, at times, of having little 'inspiration', energy or creativity, if our focus is on allowing the immense richness of Scripture to speak in all its colour and variety, the pressure is well and truly off.
6. Encourages humility in those teaching. While it can be a temptation to think that we are somehow special because we are standing at the front doing most of the talking (and, on a good day, receiving the encouragement), getting it straight that the key to preaching to the heart is simply uncovering the power and freshness of God's words helps to keep us in our place.
7. Helps us to avoid simple pragmatism. If our focus is on working consistently to enable people to encounter the God who speaks through the text, we will not feel under pressure to address every single issue and topic as it comes up in the life of the church. Conversely, working through the Bible week by week will force us to cover subjects that we wouldn't choose to address in a million years. In other words, expository preaching is the simplest, longest-lasting.
8. Drives us to preaching the gospel. Expository preaching is uniquely valuable in that it persistently drives us the Lord Jesus Christ (wherever we are in the Bible) and so 'forces' us to preach the gospel—that is, to spell out what God has already done for us in the death and resurrection of his Son, and then to move from that grace to what God asks and enables us to do. When we preach the gospel we are not simply telling people how to be good or leaving them to wallow in the overwhelming sense that they are irredeemably bad.

Reclaiming Expository Preaching

We must reclaim the method and art of expository preaching for the coming generation. No one said it would be easy. It is quite the opposite. No other method of preaching requires so much work. At the same time, no other method rewards so richly.

While the growing trend among today's preachers is toward consumer satisfaction and contemporary relevancy, we reaffirm that biblical preaching must be first directed toward divine satisfaction and kingdom relevance. Reflect carefully on Mark Steege's clarion call to expositional preaching and its note of biblical authority:

> Through our preaching the Lord seeks to change men's lives. We are to be evangelists, to awaken men to their high calling in Christ. We are to be heralds, proclaiming the messages of God to men. We are to be ambassadors, calling men to be reconciled to God. We are to be shepherds, nourishing and caring for men day by day. We are to be stewards of the mysteries of God, given men the proper Word for their every need. We are to be witnesses, telling men of all that God has done for them. We are to be overseers, urging men to live their lives to God. We are to be ministers, preparing men to minister with us to others. As we reflect on each of these phases of our work, what emphasis each gives to the importance of preaching! What a task the Lord has given us!

Although R. L. Dabney wrote over a century ago, we join him today in urging,

> . . . that the expository method (understood as that which explains extended passages of Scripture in course) be restored to that equal place which it held in the primitive and Reformed Churches; for, first, this is obviously the only natural and efficient way to do that which is the sole legitimate end of preaching, convey the whole message of God to the people.

6 Reasons Not to Abandon Expository Preaching

Some use the category "expository preaching" for all preaching that is faithful to Scripture. I distinguish expository preaching from topical preaching; textural preaching, and others, for the expository sermon must be controlled by a Scripture text or texts. Expository preaching emerges directly and demonstrably from a passage or passages of Scripture.

There are a number of reasons why expository preaching deserves to be our primary method of proclamation.

1. It is the method least likely to stray from Scripture. If you are preaching on what the Bible says about self-esteem, for example, undoubtedly you can find some useful insights. But even when you say entirely true things, you will likely abstract them from the Bible's central story line. Expository preaching keeps you to the main thing.
2. It teaches people how to read their Bibles. Especially if you're preaching a long passage, expository preaching teaches people how to think through a passage, how to understand and apply God's Word to their lives.
3. It gives confidence to the preacher and authorizes the sermon. If you are faithful to the text, you are certain your message is God's message. Regardless of what is going on in the church—whether it is growing or whether people like you—you know you are proclaiming God's truth. That is wonderfully freeing.
4. It meets the need for relevance without letting the clamor for relevance dictate the message. All true preaching is properly applied. That is of extraordinary importance in our generation. But expository preaching keeps the eternal central to the discussion.
5. It forces the preacher to handle the tough questions. You start working through text after text, and soon you hit passages on divorce, on homosexuality, on women in ministry, and you have to deal with the text.
6. It enables to the preacher to expound systematically the whole counsel of God. In the last 15 years of his life, John

Calvin expounded Genesis, Deuteronomy, Judges, Job, some psalms, 1 and 2 Kings, the major and minor prophets, the Gospels in harmony, Acts, 1 and 2 Corinthians, Galatians, Ephesians, 1 and 2 Thessalonians, and the pastoral epistles. I'm not suggesting we organize ourselves exactly the same way. But if we are to preach the whole counsel of God, we must teach the whole Bible. Other sermonic structures have their merits, but none offers our congregations more, week after week, than careful, faithful exposition of the Word of God

The Expository Sermon

Questioning expository preaching at the dawn of the twenty-first century could be compared to questioning the use of automobiles for transportation. Certainly there are other ways to get around, but the convenience, comfort and comparative cost of the automobile give it unmistakable advantages over everything else from roller blades to private helicopters. In a similar manner the advantages of the expository sermon have been touted to the present generation of preachers. The type of preaching that best carries the force of divine authority is expository preaching. A consistent and systematic exposition of the Scriptures will help restore order, end the habits of a violent society and repair damaged relationships at every level of society. There is a never dying need for the urgent return to expository preaching.

The question to be raised concerning expository preaching cannot be answered, however, simply by extolling the value of the method. In fact, it would seem possible to draw a distinction between the expository method, closely associated with the concept of hermeneutics, and the expository form, more closely associated with homiletics. This paper will suggest that the expository method, as biblical, should continue to provide the basis for sermon preparation while the expository form, as cultural, should be recognized as only one of many forms an exegetically developed sermon can take.

The Forms of Preaching in Scripture

Any discussion of biblical forms of preaching must be influenced by a presupposition concerning inspiration. Since "men moved by the Holy Spirit spoke from God," their preaching contained a significant difference from preaching today. They did not need to start from a text because they were writing the text. Discovering that they did not build their sermon on the exegesis of previously existing Scripture should not affect methodology of contemporary sermon preparation because today's preacher does not speak by inspiration. Even in the New Testament the examples of preaching must be examined in the context of the ongoing development of the inscripturation of the canon of revealed Scripture.

The admonition from Paul to Timothy to "preach the word," along with the theological presupposition that divine revelation ceased with the completion of the canon, limits today's preacher to exegeting the Biblical text. That process of exegesis commonly forms the basis for definitions of expository preaching. An investigation of the styles preaching portrayed in Scripture, if they can be separated from the content of the message preached, would conceivably allow for preaching which remains faithful to the text while assuming a variety of presentational styles.

The styles or forms which preaching assumed in the Bible do suggest a variety of methods. The prophet Jeremiah made extensive use of visuals to illustrate his words. Isiah used a poetic structure called the "taunt." Ezekiel involved himself in his proclamation, dramatically visualizing the siege of Jerusalem by his own actions. Jonah's preaching to the city of Nineveh involved a simple repetition of the message God had given to him. When Daniel read the words of Jeremiah and realized the seventy years of captivity were nearing completion, he developed a prayer based on his exegesis rather than a sermon. Many of the prophets make allusions or direct references to other prophetic writings. But the quotations are not used as the basis for a discussion the previous text. Instead they serve as appeals to authority, providing support for the arguments made by the one quoting from the other source.

Some have argued that the entire pattern of communication in the Old Testament involves an inductive rather than deductive approach. As we have seen, preaching in the Old Testament took many forms, but one form it did not take was that of exposition as commonly defined today. There appears to be no clear Old Testament example of one who organized a previously written text into discernable parts and commented on those divisions. That observation should not lead to premature conclusions, however. George Swank, while arguing for greater use of dialogue in preaching, nevertheless warns that "too rigid an adherence to historic models of prophetic preaching may insure our failure to achieve the biblical goal."

Preaching in the New Testament also assumed a great variety of forms. John Scott suggests that while there was only one church service recorded in the New Testament specifically mentioning a sermon, "there is no reason to suppose that is exceptions." Certainly many sermons are recorded in the gospels and Acts which provide examples of the preaching of Christ and the apostles.

Recent studies concerning the preaching Jesus often emphasize His inductive, or narrative, style. Certainly he was a master storyteller who instructed His listeners by repeatedly going from the concrete to the abstract, from the facts to the principles, from the data to the dictum." Parables and stories form the majority of Christ's communicative methodology. They do not, however, exclude the fact that He also used a deductive method when the occasion warranted. In the synagogue at Nazareth He read a text from Isaiah and then developed his sermon on the basis of that text.

The form which preaching assumed in both Old and New Testaments demonstrated a great variety of methodology. At the same time, because of the process of inspiration, the content of the preaching was always consistently biblical even when the sermons were not overtly drawn from previously inscripturated passages. The next question which must be answered concerns the process of preaching today. Is it possible within the umbrella of expository method to make a distinction between expository preparation or hermeneutic and expository organization or form?

Chapter 6 Exegesis & Expository Preaching

The distinctive characteristic of expository preaching is its instructional function. An explanation of the details of a given text imparts information that is otherwise unavailable to the average untrained parishioner and provides him with a foundation for Christian growth and service. The importance and centrality of thorough exegesis in preparing the expositor for this service cannot be overstated. Exegesis must itself be on a solid footing and must lead to development in supplementary fields that, in turn, provide important data for expository preaching, too. With the raw material of sermon preparation thus obtained, common-sense principles must be applied in putting the material into a form that the congregation can receive with ease and learn from.

The distinguishing mark of expository preaching, also called Bible Exposition, is the biblical interpretation communicated through the sermon. The expositor must teach his audience the meaning of the text intended by its author and understood by its original recipients. Because the original languages of the Old and New Testaments are inaccessible to almost all congregations, precise and detailed interpretations of Scripture will be also. So a Bible expositor's central responsibility is to acquaint them with these interpretations previously unknown to them. The final test of the effectiveness of Bible Exposition is how well individuals who hear the sermon can go home and read the passage with greater comprehension of its exact meaning than they could before they heard the message.

The point that differentiates expository sermons from other types is not the cleverness of their outlines or their "catchy" clichés. Neither is it the relevance of the message to everyday life. These are helpful and necessary as communicative tools and devotional helps, but they do not distinguish expository preaching from other kinds of sermons. A sermon could still be expository without them, but if the explanation of what the author meant is missing, so is the heart of Bible Exposition.

The unique contribution of Bible Exposition is its substantial enhancement of the listeners' comprehension of Scripture's intent. Such a service is the ideal way to cooperate with the Holy Spirit who inspired Scripture as He takes an improved grasp of the text's meaning and shows its applicational significance to individual listeners. That is the best avenue for building up God's people. The New Testament puts heavy emphasis on using the mind as the principle avenue to Christian growth (Rom. 12:2; 1 Pet 1:13), so the preacher should do the same.

The Critical Role of Exegesis

The responsibility on the shoulders of one who preaches this kind of message is heavy. He must have a thorough understanding of the passage to be preached before devising the mechanics for conveying his understanding to the congregation. He must be a trained exegete with a working knowledge of the biblical languages and a systematic method for using them to analyze the text.

This book cannot provide a program of exegetical training. Theological seminaries exist for this purpose. It is also beyond the present scope to formulate a system of exegesis for the Greek New Testament or Hebrew Old Testament. A few suggestive comments regarding exegesis are in order, however, so as to identify what this foundational process entails.

Accurate exegesis is ultimately dependent on the leading of the Holy Spirit in the exegete's research. Apart from His guidance, not only does the meaning of the text evade him, but also valid applications of the text will prove elusive as well (1 Cor 2:14). Since God is a God order (1 Cor 14:33, 40) and rational creatures created in His image and regenerated by His Spirit are capable of grasping divine logic, the leading of the Spirit in exegetical study will be in accord with divine reason accessible to the exegete.

Exegesis deals with the original languages of Scripture, Greek in the New Testament and Hebrew and Aramaic in the Old Testament. It does not content itself with the uncertainties of working from a translation or translations. Translations can never cover all the nuances of the original text. This is the key area in which an expositor can add to his listeners' knowledge of the text, because they usually will be limited to what they can gleam from a translation in their native tongue.

Exegesis also builds upon sound hermeneutical principles. Probably the greatest breakdown in biblical studies at the close of the twentieth century was in this field. Challenges galore have been launched against time-honored guidelines for interpreting the Bible. These challenges come from a wide variety of sources. The average pulpiteer may easily be "blown away" if he is not alert to detect the widespread aberrations that are in circulation. The importance of vigilance in this regard merits the inclusion of several illustrations of the contemporary problem among theologians.

Old Testament scholar William S. Lasor says that New Testament writers did not follow a grammatico-historical method in their use of the New Testament, so Bible interpreters today should not be limited by that method. What he failed to observe, however, is that New Testament writers received direct divine revelation whereas contemporary interpreters do not. They therefore cannot take the liberties with the text that the New Testament writers took with the Old Testament text.

Theologian Paul K. Jewett understands Paul to be inconsistent with himself regarding the role of women in the church, concluding that Paul advocates sexual equality in one of his books (Gal 3:28) and inequality in another (1 Cor 11:13). This opinion in essence dispenses with the well-known "analogy of faith" principle in biblical interpretation. It sees the Bible as inconsistent with itself.

Philosopher Anthony C. Thiselton informs us that hermeneutics is a circular process and human prejudgments make objective interpretation impossible. Such a pronouncement discourages attempts to learn the original meaning of the text and opens the floodgate for uncontrolled interpretive subjectivism. At best it has the effect of destroying the goal of objectivity that traditional Protestant interpretation has always pursued, and at worst it signals an end of rationality in studying the Bible.

Missiologist Krikor Haleblian advocates the principle of contextualization whereby each culture is allowed to form its own system of hermeneutics based on the praxis of ministry in meeting its own peculiar needs. Yet if each culture formulated its own principles of interpretation to make the Bible mean something conceived as necessary for its own isolated situation, objective control of the Bible means is terminated. The connotation for the original recipients of the writings has become completely irrelevant.

I. Howard Marshall, redaction critic, cites as non-historical a number of sayings attributed to Christ in the Gospels, viewing them to be later additions added by the church for clarifying purposes. Traditional interpretation, on the other hand, views the gospels as containing accurate historical data about Jesus.

The circulation of subtle hermeneutical variations such as the above has contributed heavily to the interpretive confusion prevalent in some churches in the 1990's. These can become a serious hindrance to accurate exegesis and ultimately to expository preaching if they are not shunned.

Exegesis also presupposes a text that is fixed through a valid application of text-critical principles. The canons of the Old and New Testament are also in place and are the object of the expositor's interpretive efforts. A thorough background knowledge of authorship, date of writing, destination, and the like i.e., the field called Biblical Introduction regarding the book under scrutiny is also a necessary foundation for exegesis.

Exegesis itself incorporates a study of individual words, their backgrounds, their derivation, their usage, their synonyms, their antonyms, their figurative usages, and other lexical aspects. Elaboration on Greek and Hebrew words in pulpit exposition is by far the most frequently encountered homiletically use of exegesis, but it is only a small beginning. Of at least equal, and probably greater, importance is the way the words are joined in sentences, paragraphs, sections, etc. This area of "syntax," as it is called is too frequently overlooked. Yet only a full appreciation of syntactical relationships can provide a specific understanding of the flow of thought that the Spirit intended in His revelation through the human writers of the Scripture.

A thorough familiarity with the historical background of each book is also imperative. Without this, the meaning to readers in the original setting is beyond reach of the expositor, and hence, of his audience, too.

The church of the twenty-first century is to be beneficiary of a rich treasure of Bible teaching published throughout the centuries of the Christian era. Gifted teachers whom Christ has placed in the church have preserved their interpretations on the printed page. It behooves the exegete to take full advantage of these God-given sources of enrichment in acquiring a keener mastery of the meaning he must teach.

It is futile to assume that these gifted writers never disagree in their interpretations. It is the challenge of the Bible expositor under the guidance of the Spirit to evaluate each of the conflicting opinions in light of sound hermeneutical principles and exegetical procedures and to settle on the one that he feels to be correct. That is what he will preach to his congregation as the true interpretation.

After the tedious process of exegetical analysis, the expositor will have amassed an immense amount of data, much of it technical, but he should also have arrived at a detailed comprehension of the Scripture's interpretation. He must now select from this massive accumulation of material the parts that are most significant to transmit to his listeners.

A major precaution to observe is not preaching exegetical data from the pulpit. Because the expositor has been enlightened so much by what he has discovered, his initial impulse may be to pass on to his people the excitement of his discovery in the same terminology as he received it. This is a major mistake. Very few in the pew have a background sufficient to enable them to comprehend the kind of technical data derived from exegesis. So the minister of the Word must adapt his explanations to suit the vocabulary and interest level of those to whom he speaks. He must develop a technique of conveying in the language of a non-specialist what he has learned from his specialized analysis. How he does so may vary. It may be through paraphrase, description, analogy, illustration, or in a multitude of other ways. Yet he must explain the text in a way that is interesting and comprehensive to his people. This explanation is the core of Bible Exposition.

Auxiliary fields of study

Yet Bible exposition includes much more. In a logical development of theological and ministerial disciplines, it is built upon other fields of investigation besides just exegesis. These other fields of study are based on exegesis too, but they amplify exegesis by stipulating different ways of applying it.

> (1) Biblical and Systematic Theology. One cannot reach an accurate perception of God and His works without basing it on a correct interpretation of the Bible. It is vital that these theological perspectives be incorporated into expository preaching at appropriate times.
>
> (2) Church History. The doctrinal and ethical development of the Christian church from century to century can be evaluated properly only through the eyes of the Bible correctly understood. Lessons learned by earlier generations of believers, both good and bad, made excellent sermon illustrations. They also provoke imitation of exemplary behavior of saints of the past and guard Christians from repeating the mistakes of those who have gone before.
>
> (3) Apologetics. The New Testament is clear in its instruction to Christians about defending the faith against attack (Phil

1:7; 1 Pet 3:15-16). Philosophies of religion vary widely because the nature of philosophy lends itself so readily to mere human reasoning. Logic is not necessarily secular, however. Under the control of conclusions reached in biblical exegesis, apologetical methodologies can apply sound logic in responding to those who attack the integrity of the Bible and the Christian faith. Well-rounded expository preaching will incorporate these biblically oriented answers whenever necessary.

(4) Applicational ministries. Also based on exegesis is a wide assortment of services in which the principles of Scripture rightly interpreted are applied to human experience. Practical uses of the Bible are multiple and varied, but they must be controlled. Correct interpretation is the only suitable control. If the meaning of the text in its original setting does not regulate application, applications become extremely subjective and essentially invalid.

(a) Homiletics. The field of sermon preparation and delivery is broad, but the structure of the sermon and the motivation for its delivery must be rooted in the text. All too often, secular methodologies and ideas that are only human have been determinative of the shape of a sermon. If thorough exegesis is the foundation of a message, this will not happen.

(b) Counseling. The counsel that the Bible prescribes is administered most effectively through members of Christ's body who possess the gift of exhortation. This gift along with the gift of teaching forms an effective combination that makes up what we call preaching (Rom 12:7-8). Exhortation, or "encouragement" as the Greek term can also be rendered, includes rebuke to the wayward Christian and comfort to one beset by grief. It covers the broad spectrum of advice on how to live the Christian life. Unfortunately much of what passes itself off as Christian counseling is more secular than it is biblical. That is because it is not on a solid exegetical footing. Expository preaching does well to include the right kinds of application to the assembled group, just as it should be done on an individual or small-group basis, i.e., a counseling situation.

(c) Christian Education. Education that is really Christian will derive from exegesis. That is true of secular educational methodologies will not necessary apply in efforts to impart biblical truth. For example, the secular assumption that something must be experienced before it can be learned is the reverse sequence of what the Bible prescribes. Doctrine precedes and determines practical experience in the biblical pattern. Utilization of biblical principles of education in messages whose purpose is to teach the meaning of Scripture is another supporting element of Bible Exposition.

(d) Administration. Unfortunately many have attempted to incorporate secular administrative philosophies into local-church operations. Pragmatism has often been given as a reason for this: "If it works in the business world, use it." Such reasoning is ethically inferior, however. The biblical dimension in administration gives first attention to this principle: "Is it right according to Scripture?" The Bible has much to say about how to rule or govern. In fact, it designates a special gift of the Spirit for carrying out this function (Rom 12:8; 1 Cor 12:28). Since under normal circumstances the Bible expositor will serve his church in an administrative capacity, it can be expected that exegetically based principles of leadership will sometimes be reflected in his preaching.

(e) Missions and Evangelism. Missions and evangelism are proper goals in Christian service, but the means used to reach these goals are not always so proper. Even here manmade schemes have replaced scripturally prescribed methods of winning lost people to Christ. When missionary methods and evangelistic techniques are based on what the Bible teaches, however, both the means and the end are God-honoring. Hence exegesis must also be the footing on Christian outreach is built. Expository preaching will in turn build on missions and evangelism rightly construed in those aspects of the sermon devoted to bringing an offer of salvation.

(f) Social Issues. How Christians should involve themselves in combatting the ills of society and helping meet the multiplied needs of the world as a whole must stem from an accurate understanding of the Word too. Scripture clarifies certain causes that are very worthy and supplies outlines of how God's people can help alleviate suffering and rectify injustice. Christians have responsibilities as citizens in the world. The preacher who features Bible Exposition should amplify these responsibilities when they are appropriate to the passage he is developing.

Practical Suggestions for Expository Preachers

The preceding text reflects that Exegesis and Bible Exposition are not the same. Exegesis may be defined as the critical or technical application of hermeneutical principles to a biblical text in the original languages with a view to the exposition or declaration of its meaning. Since exegesis leads to exposition but is not identical with it, a few suggestions about how to make the transition from one to the other are in order.

As in the process of exegesis, it is also true of the transition from that point to sermon preparation and delivery that the leading of the Spirit of God is indispensable. This is the only way of accomplishing the work of God in the lives of people through preaching (cf. 1 Thess 1:5). The preacher must be a man in whom the Spirit has been and is at work before he can be an instrument through whom the Spirit will work in the lives of others as he preaches.

A warning issued above is worth repeating. A transition from exegesis to Bible Exposition is mandatory. Pulpiteers who are fluent enough to expound the technical data of exegesis and still hold the attention of an average congregation have been and are extremely rare. The information gleaned from exegesis must be put into a format that fits the understanding of the person in the pew and is applicable to his situation.

Exegesis must also be expanded to embody other fields of doctrinal and ethical relevance. A preacher need not include every field in every sermon he preaches. These are areas that may be introduced as the nature of the passage and the occasion of the sermon require.

Beyond these general suggestions, some specific pointers may be beneficial. These miscellaneous guidelines are the ones that have seemed most apropos to this writer in over ten years of personal preaching and listening to other preachers.

(1) The preacher should review the results of the exegetical study and select parts that will most typically represent his detailed interpretation of the passage. Time will not allow him to include everything he has learned, so he must select what is most important for his congregation to hear.
(2) In his sparing use of technical terminology that may be unintelligible to his audience, the expositor should not shy away from referring occasionally to Greek words that lie behind the English translation. When doing so, he can help his cause by comparing the Greek term to an English word derived from it. The expositor must be careful not to overuse Greek terminology.
(3) The Bible expositor should describe as best he can the thoughts of the human writer of Scripture that resulted in his writing what he did. These subjective impressions were products of the Holy Spirit's inspiration and are key elements in a precise understanding of accurate interpretation. A writer's logical de-

velopments are best captured through close attention to features of syntactical exegesis referred to above. The use of conjunctions in the New Testament is particularly strategic in cultivating sensitivity to movement of thought in the text. This type of information is most effectively passed on to the audience in the form of descriptions or paraphrases of the text.

(4) Public presentation is not the proper forum to resolve in detail difficult interpretive problems, but an expositor's awareness of the problems should be reflected in his presentation. After surveying the possible viewpoints, he should include one or two good reasons why he has selected a solution as the correct one. If he were to skip past a problem in the text without noticing it, he would shake the confidence of those listeners who may be aware of the problem. Tough issues should not be left unsolved, no matter how difficult they are. If the preacher is indecisive, his indecision will be multiplied into outright confusion among his hearers who have nowhere else to turn for an answer. They have nothing comparable to the tools of a trained exegete to grapple with obscure passages. With particularly difficult matters, the expositor does well to admit publicly his personal struggle in reaching a decision, but he should nevertheless not shy away from expressing his own preferred answer in each problem passage.

(5) A careful personal translation of the passage to be preached based on thorough exegesis is a primary prerequisite in sermon preparation. In producing it, the preacher should read the text repeatedly in the original language and then turn to English translations for further enlightenment on how others have rendered the words. As opportunity arises, the expositor's personal translation may be made available to the congregation in a published form.

(6) The sermon's proposition and outline should have an interpretational rather than applicational orientation. This reinforces the central purpose of the sermon as a teaching device. It is primary that listeners should carry away an understanding of the text's *meaning*. Suggestions of practical effects on Christian living are quite appropriate in the message, but without being founded on the original intention of the author, they will be

short-lived. Besides, long after the sermon is over, the Holy Spirit will add to these suggested practical lessons others of an individual nature as people reflect on what the text means. Preaching is first and foremost a service to the mind as groundwork for a service to the heart. The will and emotions are influenced in a lasting way only in proportion to the degree that the mind has learned correct biblical teaching and the level of behavior consonant with that teaching.

(7) In an ideal situation the sequence within the sermon structure should follow the sequence of the passage of Scripture being treated, but sometimes the nature of the passage and/or the occasion of the sermon may require a sermon outline that draws upon emphases within the passage in a non-sequential order. The latter approach may sometimes be the best pedagogical tool for helping the audience to grasp the fundamental thrust of the passage. Whenever the out-of-sequence is used, a tracing of the passage's sequential flow should be included in the introduction or elsewhere in the sermon. A combined emphasis from the sequential summary and the text's underlying principles tendered non-sequentially will greatly benefit the hearers when they are reviewing the passage privately after the sermon.

(8) An expositor should make every effort not to preach preconceived notions of what a given text may say. His sacred trust is to let the text speak for itself and not impose on it what he thinks or wishes it said. Much too frequently a preacher conceives of what his congregation's need are and rushes naively to a text to support his conception. The results are tragic for the exegetical process, and beyond this, the preacher's prime reason for standing before people has suffered abuse.

(9) The proper choice of an English translation on which to base a sermon is important, but whatever version is chosen, the preacher will have to correct or clarify the translation during the message. He must be careful to limit these corrections, perhaps to only two or three, during the process of a message for fear of shaking the confidence of his listeners in the Bible they hold in their hands. After all, part of his goal is cultivating a hunger among his people to study the Bible privately. Too many criti-

cisms of that Bible will undermine their dependence on a given translation and fuel a "what's the use?" attitude on their side.

(10)   Contemporary preaching is best done by people who possess the spiritual gifts of teaching and exhortation (Rom 12:7-8; 1 Cor 12:28-29; Eph 4:11). It combines a ministry primarily to the human intellect with one addressed primarily to the will. Teaching provides instruction in doctrine which is the basis for exhortations on how to live more consistently for Christ. No two people have these combined gifts in equal strengths, nor do they have the gifts in the same proportions. So each person is completely unique and need not try to produce an exact imitation of some else's preaching. Among prospective preachers in particular the tendency is to observe a preacher with a strong "charisma" an indescribable appeal and attractiveness with listeners and to try to imitate him. This is a mistake because no two members of the body of Christ have identical functions or were meant to be clones of one another.

(11)   The speaker should have a general idea of the average level of comprehension of those addressed. He should gear most of his remarks just below that level, but periodically he should rise above that level a bit. This will challenge his people and keep them from getting bored with hearing so much that they already know. If he stays above that level too much, they will become frustrated and lose interest because they are in the dark about what is being preached. Balance is the key.

(12)   Every expository message should teach something that recipients did not already know before hearing the sermon. To some congregations unaccustomed to an expository ministry this may be uncomfortable at first. They have not come to the church service to be instructed because sermons they have heard in the past have consisted of a series of personal experiences or a string of platitudes without a firm biblical basis, and not of instruction about the meaning of the text. There orientation has been reflected in the oft-repeated philosophy, "Our problem isn't that we don't know enough, but that we don't put what we do know into practice." This ill-conceived philosophy assumes that knowing and doing are antithetical i.e. an "either-or" pair when in reality they are not. The real situation is better

stated, "Our problem is that we don't know enough *and* that we don't put what we do know into practice." Instruction must be the prime objective if long-lasting, spiritually-improved behavior is to result. Meeting the challenge of Bible Exposition to teach the previously unknown is facilitated by the expositor's familiarity with the original text. Usually he will have more than he can teach in his allotted time. As the saying goes, "His sermon barrel will never run dry."

(13) The preacher of God's Word should take care not to overload his congregation. The average Christian can digest only so much at one sitting, particularly when he is being taught previously unfamiliar material. The messenger must be very sensitive to the capacity of those who sit under his ministry and govern his teaching accordingly.

(14) How much a Bible expositor can teach effectively in one sermon is the function of a wide variety of factors. It will depend upon his combination-giftedness in teaching and exhortation, the nature of the sermon text, his method of preparation, the attention-span of his hearers, and other factors. As a general rule, with most congregations in the American culture, the first fifteen-to-twenty minutes is the best time to emphasize teaching in a message. After this, listeners tend to become mentally fatigued, so to speak, and added effort is necessary to hold their attention. More applications of the text and illustrations of its principles are good ways to spark attentiveness. This does not mean that the first half of the sermon must be devoid of applications and illustrations, or that the last half must completely ignore teaching. It is rather a matter of the proportional emphasis to be given to each in successive parts of the sermon.

(15) In expository preaching, teaching of the "not already known" should be mingled with what listeners do already know or what they can glean for themselves from reading an English translation. This familiar material furnishes them with a point of reference to which they can relate the new instruction received. Without this anchor they have no way to assimilate the message with their already formulated Christian beliefs. With

this reference point their broad comprehension of Christian doctrine as a whole can be expanded.

(16)   The expository should avoid the pitfall of sensationalism. The temptation to gear one's message for novelty is strong. Forcing upon the original text a spectacular connotation that it was never intended to convey is all too common. A preacher may do this sort of thing for the shock-effect and consequent popularity it produces. If he opts for this route to gain applause or acceptance by his listeners, he has abused his responsibility and privilege as a proclaimer of God's Word. The line separating the selfish motives of a sensation-seeker and the unselfish motives of a humble attempt to maintain audience attention is sometimes very fine. God's servant must be careful not to cross that line in the wrong direction.

Chapter 7 Creating the Expository Sermon

Doctrine, i.e., teaching is the preacher's chief business. To teach men truth, or to quicken what they already know into freshness and power, is the preacher's great means of doing good. The facts and truths which belong to the Scripture account for sin, Providence, and redemption, form the staple of all scriptural preaching. But these truths ought not simply to have place after a desultory and miscellaneous fashion in our preaching.

The entire body of Scripture teaching upon any particular subject, when collected and systematically arranged, has come to be called the "doctrine" of Scripture on that subject and in this sense we ought to preach much on the doctrines of the Bible. We all regard it as important that the preacher should himself have sound views of doctrine; is it not also important that he should lead his congregation to have just views?

Martyn Lloyd-Jones, a great preacher of London in the mid-twentieth century, knew that structuring the sermon is one of our most difficult homiletical tasks:

> The preparation of sermons involves sweat and labour. It can be difficult at times to get all this matter that you have found in the Scriptures into an outline. It is like a ... blacksmith making shoes for a horse; you have to keep on putting the material into the fire and on the anvil and hit it again and again with the hammer. Each time it is a bit better, but not quite right; so you put it back again and again until you are satisfied with it or can do no better. This is the most grueling part of the preparation of a sermon; but at the same time it is a most fascinating and a most glorious occupation. (Preachers and Preaching, 80)

When pastors begin their sermon prep (and unfortunately, sometimes when they end their sermon prep), the text often seems to be, as Hamlet said, "words, words, words." The relationships among the words—

the ideas presented—are hard to discern and even harder to package for the congregation. This chapter is to help us make sense of the words and structure them in a way that makes sense to the listeners. As homiletical blacksmiths, five strokes of the hammer help us structure our sermons.

Defining the Expository Sermon

James Braga defines an expository sermon as one in which a more or less extended portion of Scripture is interpreted in relation to one theme or central idea. The bulk of the material for the sermon is drawn directly from the passage and the outline consists of a series of progressive ideas centered on that one main idea.

Haddon Robinson's definition emphasizes the content base of sermon preparation, but goes on to describe a method of linear, propositional organization which he also calls expository preaching. Only incidentally does he refer to other forms and even then he defines them in relationship to his primary method of logical organization. "In a narrative sermon, as in any other sermon, a major idea continues to be supported by other ideas, but the content supporting the points is drawn directly from the incidents in the story. In other words the details of the story are woven together to make a point and all the points develop the central idea of the sermon.

An expository sermon is a discourse based on a portion of Scripture, occupied mainly with exposition, wholly restricted in the outline to the chosen passage, and delivered with a view to persuasion.

The Expository Process

Discussing the biblical foundations and the definition of expository preaching, while essential, is relatively easy. The real challenge comes when one has to move from the classroom to the weekly pulpit. Unless the preacher understands clearly the expository process, he will never achieve his potential in the craft of expository preaching. The expository process consists of four elements:

1. Preparing the expositor
   Since God should be the source of expository messages, one who delivers such a message should enjoy intimate communion with God. This is the only way the message can be given with greatest accuracy, clarity and passion.

   Seven areas of preparation qualify the preacher to stand in the pulpit and declare, "Thus saith Lord!"

   a. The preacher must be a truly regenerated believer in Jesus Christ. He must be a part of God's redeemed family (John 1:12-13). If a man is to deliver a personal message from the Heavenly Father effectively, he must be a legitimate spiritual son, or the message will inevitably be distorted.
   b. The preacher must be appointed and gifted by God to the teaching/preaching ministry (Eph. 4:11-16; 1 Tim 3:2). Unless a man is divinely enabled to proclaim, he will be inadequate, possessing only human ability.
   c. The preacher must be inclined and trained to be a student of God's Word. Otherwise, he cannot carry out the mandate of 2 Tim 2:15 to "cut straight" the Word of God's truth.
   d. The preacher must be a mature believer who demonstrates a consistently godly character (1 Tim 3:2-3).
   e. The preacher must be dependent upon God the Holy Spirit for divine insight and understanding of God's Word (1 Cor 2:12-13). Without the Spirit's illumination and power, the message will be relatively impotent.
   f. The preacher must be in constant prayerful communion with God to receive the full impact of the Word (Ps 119:18). The obvious one to consult for clarification is the original author.

g. The preacher must first let the developing message sift through his own thinking and life before he can preach it. Ezra provides the perfect model (Ezra 7:10).

2. Processing and Principlizing the Biblical Text(s)
A man in tune with God's Spirit and Word is ready to begin a process to discover not only what God originally meant by what He said, but also appropriate principles and applications for today.

   a. Processing the biblical text
   A man cannot hope to preach effectively without first having worked diligently and thoroughly through the biblical text. This is the only way the expositor can acquire God's message.

   b. Principlizing the biblical text
   Preaching does not stop with understanding ancient languages, history, culture, and customs. Unless the centuries can be bridged with contemporary relevance in the message, then the preaching experience differs little from a classroom encounter. One must first process the text for original meaning and then principlize the text for current applicability. One's study falls short of the goal if this step is omitted or slighted.

3. Pulling the Expository Message Together
At the third stage the expositor has finished his deep study and asks, "How can I blend my findings in such a way that my flock will understand the Bible and its requirements for their lives today?" In a sense, the art of exposition commences here.

Nolan Howington uses a graphic description to relate exegesis and exposition: "Thus an exegete is like a diver bringing up pearls from the ocean bed; an expositor is like the jeweler who arrays them in orderly fashion and in proper relation to each other."

Titles, outlines, introductions, illustrations, and conclusions enter the process at this state. The message moves from the raw materials mined by exegesis to the finished product of exposition, which the hearers hopefully will find interesting, convincing, and compelling. The key to this step is remembering what distinguishes exposition: explaining the text, especially parts that are to understand or apply. It is equally important to remember not only the text, but the audience as well.

F. B. Meyer offers this advice when thinking of the listeners and what sermonic form the message will take:

> There are five considerations that must be met in every successful sermon. There should be an appeal to the Reason, to the Conscience, to the Imagination, to the Emotions, and to the Will; and for each of these there is no method as serviceable as systematic exposition.

4. Preaching the Exposition
The final decision to be made by the expositor relates to his preaching mode, whether from memory or from notes. This step is perhaps the most neglected in preparation by those committed to true exposition. Too often expositors assume that proper work done in the study will ensure that the pulpit will take care for itself. It is true that there is no substitute for hard work in the study, but equally hard work in the pulpit will reward both the preacher and the flock to a much greater degree.

Ministers do not get enough of result in the attention, satisfaction and delight of their hearers for the work they do; and the failure is in the vehicle of communication between the study and the congregation that is to say, in the delivery of the sermon. James Stalker pleads for more work to show for the coal consumed.

At this point of delivery, it is essential for the expositor to be clear in his purpose. Otherwise, the message preached may be far afield from the message studied and the message of Scripture.

The purpose of preaching is not to stir people to action while bypassing their minds, so that they never see what reason God gives them for doing what the preacher requires of them (that is manipulation); nor is the purpose to stock people's minds with truth, no matter how vital and clear, which then lies fallow and does not become the see-bed and source of changed lives (that is academicism)... The purpose of preaching is to inform, persuade, and call forth an appropriate response to the God whose message and instruction are delivered.

Also of importance is the language used in communicating the message. It should be clear, understandable, picturesque, and most of all biblical.

William Ayer warned us decades ago to adhere to Biblical terminology. Much modern preaching has taken a psychological and sociological turn. It is mysterious and mystical. It sets forth psychiatric ideas, often using the terms of the psychiatrist rather than those of the Christian evangelist. It speaks of repression, fixations, traumas, neuroses, and syndromes, world without end. Ayer claimed that in the main these are not terms that the Holy Spirit can use effectively.

Another crucial matter is the dynamics of speech, i.e. audience relationship and communicative effectiveness. According to Vines and Allen, effective communication from the pulpit must be informed by Aristotle's rhetorical triad of logos, ethos, and pathos. This involves a thorough knowledge of the subject matter and here is where there is no substitute for thorough exegesis. It involves a thorough knowledge of the speaker-audience dynamic such that the preacher must speak from integrity and his audience must know of his sincerity and genuineness. Finally it involves knowledge of people and how they respond to the spoken word.

Above all, the expositor must expound the Word like Paul did in Corinth (1 Cor 2:15). He did not come as a clever orator or scholarly genius; he did not arrive with his own message; he did not preach with personal confidence in his own strength. Rather, Paul preached the testimony of God and Christ's death, and this will well-placed confidence in God's power to make the message life-changing. Unless this kind of wholesale dependence on God marks the modern expositor's preaching his exposition will lack the divine dimension that only God can provide.

In summary, of the four steps of the complete expository experience preparing the expositor, processing and principlizing the biblical text, pulling the expository message together, and preaching the exposition no phase can be omitted without seriously jeopardizing the truthfulness or usefulness of God's Word mediated through the expositor.

Features of an Expository Sermon

(1) The text of an expository sermon provides the material for all the divisions and subdivisions. But, not only is the division structure provided by the text; the elaboration, or exposition, is also mainly derived from the passage of Scripture chosen for the text.

(2) The text of an expository sermon is usually longer than the text of a textual or a topical sermon. In fact, the text will usually be a paragraph or a chapter, and sometimes, it will be a whole book of the Bible. However, occasional one will find a single verse so full and meaningful that it will be sufficient to provide all the material for a sermon.

(3) Furthermore, the expository sermon is a treatment of the passage of Scripture, while the topical and textual sermons are treatments of the subject though the textual sermon gets its main headings from the text, it is really a treatment of a subject as suggested by a text and the subject is the principle thing. An expository sermon will have a subject, but the subject is subordinate to the text; the text is the principal thing.

(4) Finally, in expository sermon, the Scripture passage is chosen first, and the subject is derived afterward, while in the other sermon types the subject usually selected first, and the Scripture text is found afterward. The reason for this that expository sermons are most frequently preached in series of courses and consequently the individual sermon is selected because it develops a pre-selected

subject. Of course, expository sermons may be preached as occasional sermons as well as in series, but even when this is the case, the Scripture passage is selected because it contains a noteworthy story, parable, conversation, incident or biographical sketch or it is one of the more familiar chapters which are well known for their appeal or practical application.

State the Exegetical Outline

Clear structure of the sermon depends on crystal clear understanding of the flow of thought in the passage. Do not rush this foundational step in your exegesis. Summarize the flow of thought in your text. We call this the exegetical outline, and it is part of basic exegesis. If you have gotten away from that discipline, get back to it. Charting the flow of thought with a mechanical layout, grammatical diagram, or semantic structural analysis is an indispensable step in creating an expository sermon. Simply identifying a general theme is not enough to reveal author intention. Laying out the major ideas and their relationships will help you identify the unifying core of the text, what Haddon Robinson calls the exegetical idea.

Once you articulate that idea, then you can turn it into your sermon's "big idea." In essay writing this is called the thesis. In public speaking it is called the central idea. The big idea is the distilled essence of the message. Compare the exegetical idea (the text's central truth) and the big idea (the sermon's central truth):

Exegetical Idea	Big Idea
Purpose—to summarize the passage in a single sentence	Purpose—to communicate the message of the passage in a single sentence so that it aids comprehension and lodges in memory
Sounds like a commentary	Sounds like a proverb
As long as necessary for accuracy and thoroughness	Fifteen words of fewer

Third person	First or second person
Past tense	Present tense
Example from Psalm 32:	Example from Psalm 32:
• The psalmist praised God for the forgiveness he received after confessing his sin, because blessing attends the one whose sins are covered by God, but woes attend the one who tries to cover his own sin.	• Cover or be covered

Every sermon should have a big idea for two reasons. The first relates to sound hermeneutics. Conservative exegetes believe in authorial intention—that the biblical authors intended to convey ideas to their readers. In any thought unit such as a paragraph in an epistle or a scene in a narrative, the author wanted to get a point across. To be sure, texts have many ideas, but our job in exegesis is to discern how those relate to each other. They swirl around a central point. Texts are not a random hodgepodge. Stating the exegetical idea helps us to articulate authorial intention.

The second reason relates to communication. Sermons are most effective when they are laser focused. When the preacher cuts extraneous fat, listeners comprehend clearly. Reducing the essence of the sermon to one idea will increase its impact.

As you outline the text's flow of ideas, you can expect to see the following patterns of thought, common to human experience:
- Problem-Solution
- Cause-Effect
- Contrast (Not this, but this)
- Chronology (First this happened, then this, then this)
- Promises-Fulfillment
- Lesser to Greater
- Argument-Proof
- Explanation-Application
- Principle-Example/Amplification

Other patterns undoubtedly exist, and once you train your mind to think in logical categories like these presented here, discerning flow of thought becomes second nature. Some of the patterns above use inductive reasoning, and some use deductive reasoning. Induction starts with particulars and moves toward a conclusion or principle. The first six patterns are inductive. Deduction starts with the conclusion or axiom and then explains, proves, or applies that idea. The last three are deductive.

Here is an exegetical outline for <u>James 4:13-17</u>, with commentary on the flow of thoughts in italics:

I. Some of James' readers boasted about tomorrow. (v.13)

Effect: The passage begins inductively with an example of boasting. This is the effect of the cause James will identify later in the passage (arrogance). The author places a hypothetical speech in the mouths of the readers to show them what arrogance sounds like.

II. James rebukes such boasting (v. 14)

Contrast: In contrast to the wealth of knowledge implied in the boastful opening speech, the readers actually know little. They do not know the future. They are as fragile as mist. The logical flow from v. 13 to v. 14 is contrast: not this, but this.

III. James contrasts boastful speech with submissive speech (v.15)

Contrast continued: The author continues with the logic of contrast by creating another hypothetical speech. This second speech shows proper words that are submissive and humble, in contrast with the opening speech.

IV. The readers boast because they are arrogant. (V. 16a)

Cause: The author has described and illustrated the effect (boasting), and now he reveals the cause: arrogance. Westerners normally think in terms of cause-effect, but the reverse, effect-cause, is also possible.

V. Boasting is evil, and anyone who knows this, but persists in boasting, sins. (v. 16b-17)

Summary: James pulls the camera back to present the broad landscape. He ends by summarizing the previous exhortation about boasting. (Another possibility is that he provides further arguments why the readers should not boast.)

Here is an exegetical outline for <u>Psalm 32:</u>

I. Blessed is the one whom the Lord has forgiven (vv.1-2)

Announcement of Theme: David summarizes the whole psalm with this headline.

II. When the author tried to cover his own sins, the Lord disciplined him. (vv. 3-4)

Problem: David describes the trouble his silence brought— the Lord's heavy hand of discipline. Transition says that this psalm grew out of David's personal experience—his sins of adultery and murder, and his attempt to cover his own sins. After the announcement of the theme, he describes how miserable he was when he refused to confess.

III. Then the author confessed, and God forgave (v. 5)

Solution: After experiencing the discipline of God, David finally confessed and experienced the blessings described in vv. 1-2. The logical (and somewhat chronological) flow moves from trouble to grace, problem to solution.

IV. The author urges others to follow his example and experience God's deliverance (vv. 6-11)

Exhortation: David exhorts the readers to learn from his experience. The wicked experience sorrow, but the love of God surrounds the ones who trust him. Therefore, confess!

Rephrase (and Possibly Re-order) the Points as a Homiletical Outline

Using John Stott's metaphor of "standing between two words," the exegetical outline resides in the world of the text, and the homiletical outline resides in the world of the listener. Compare:

Exegetical Outline	Homiletical Outline
Past tense	Present tense
Third person	First or second person
Summarizes the author's thought	Summarizes your thought *from* the text *for* the congregation
Follows the textual order exactly	Usually follows the textual order, but can also follow "thought order"

We will illustrate the last item in this chart later, but first let's examine the top three items. In the examples that follow, notice that the outline no longer sounds like a commentary ("James told his readers to do such and such", "David did this or that"). Rather, it sounds like a living soul addressing living souls.

Here is the homiletical outline from James 4:13-18:

I. Sometimes we boast about tomorrow. (v. 13)

II. We should not do this, because our knowledge is limited and our days short (v. 14)

III.   *Big Idea*: Rather than boasting, we should speak with humility and submission to God's will. (v. 15)

IV.   The cause of our boasting is arrogance. (v. 16a)

V.   Now that you know this, if you continue to boast, you sin. (16b-17)

Here is a homiletical outline from Psalm 32:
I.   *Big Idea (Summary)*: Blessed is the one whom the Lord has forgiven. (vv. 1-2)
II.   *Problem*: When we refuse to confess our sins, we bake in the oven of discipline. (vv. 3-4)

III.   *Solution*: Confess your sins, and God will forgive. (v. 5)

IV.   *Exhortation*: Listen to God's wisdom and experience God's deliverance. (vv. 6-11)

To return to the issue above—the issue of textual order and thought order—consider this helpful example from Donald Sunukjian:

> *Textual order*: "Don't get mad when the paperboy throws your paper in the bushes." The arrangement is *response* (don't get mad) to *cause* (the paperboy throws your paper in the bushes).
>
> *Thought order*: A sermon from this "text" could rearrange the textual order into the more natural thought order of *cause-response*. This would help the listeners follow the sequence of ideas. Thus:
>
> I.   *Cause*: Sometimes the paperboy throws your paper in the bushes.
>
> II.   *Response*: When that happens, don't get mad.

Although expository preachers usually adhere to textual order, rearranging the points of the expository outline can sometimes help us stand between two worlds. Rearrangement can help us clarify the meaning of the text.

Here are two examples from the texts above. First is a homiletical outline from James 4:13-17, rearranged for inductive order:

    I.   Our knowledge is limited, and our days are short. (v. 14)

          Transition: Yet ...

    II.   In our arrogance we boast. (vv. 13, 16a)

          Transition: Therefore ...

    III.   Such boasting is sin. (16b-17)

          Transition: In contrast ...

    IV.   *Big Idea:* We should speak with humility and submission to God's will. (v. 15)

The flow of thought in the outline above moves inductively. Starting with the assertion that we are fragile creatures, limited and ephemeral, the sermon's final point is the big idea. The sermon has driven toward the big idea.

Another homiletical outline could be arranged deductively, stating the big idea first. For example, here is a homiletical outline from James 4:13-17 rearranged for deductive thought order:

    I.   *Big Idea:* We should speak with humility and submission to God's will (v. 15)

          Transition: Why? Because ...

II. Our knowledge is limited, and our days are short. (v. 14)

Transition: Yet ...

III. In our arrogance we boast (vv. 13, 16a)

Transition: Therefore ...

IV. Such boasting is a sin. (16b-17)

Here is a homiletical outline for Psalm 32 rearranged for deductive thought order:

I. *Big Idea (Solution)*: Confess your sins. (v. 5)

Transition: As a result ...

II. *Result*: Experience God's deliverance (vv. 1-2)

Transition: In contrast ...

III. *Problem*: When we refuse to confess our sins, we bake in the oven of discipline. (vv. 3-4)

Transition: Therefore ...

IV. *Exhortation*: Listen to God's wisdom, and experience God's deliverance. (vv. 6-11)

The example above states the big idea early in the sermon and then returns to it in the last point. The next example, a homiletical outline of Psalm 32 rearranged for inductive thought order, saves the big idea until the last point:

I. *Problem*: When we refuse to confess our sins, we bake in the oven of discipline. (vv. 3-4)

Transition: In contrast, what we truly desire is ...

II. *Contrast*: When we allow God to cover our sins, we know peace. (vv. 1-2)

Transition: Therefore ...

III. *Big Idea (Solution)*: Confess your sins (v. 5)

Transition: As a result ...

IV. *Exhortation*: Listen to God's wisdom, and experience God's deliverance. (vv. 6-11)

The examples above demonstrate that expository preachers have latitude when it comes to structure. Our normal procedure, once again, is to follow the exegetical outline when creating the homiletical outline, but pastoral wisdom will sometimes suggest that we arrange the points into a different order.

Develop the Points

Now that you have summarized the text's flow of thought and have rephrased (and possibly reordered) the points, put flesh on the bones. Develop the ideas by addressing the questions the listeners will ask. If they ask:

<u>Listeners' Question</u>	<u>Preachers' Response</u>
What does that mean?	*You must explain. The preacher takes the stance of a teacher.*
Is that true?	*You must defend/prove. The preacher takes the stance of an apologist.*
So what?	*You must apply. The preacher takes the stance of an equipper or exhorter, urging behavioral response.*

This stage of structuring a clear and effective sermon demands audience analysis. You have to know the listeners' level of knowledge, belief, and submission to the text. Listen to the points of our outline through the ears of your listeners.

Furthermore, these three developmental questions are psychologically sequential. That is, people will often believe what has been clearly explained to them, and they will often do what they believe. Conversely, they are unlikely to believe what they do not understand; and they will not act upon what they do not believe. I have discovered that many people will respond to the gospel in faith and repentance if we simply explain it clearly. But if we cloud their understanding, they will neither believe nor respond.

Understanding—when well established, often leads to ...
Agreeing—when well-established, often leads to ...
Responding

We fulfill all three functions—explaining, proving, and applying—by taking the truth to every SEAT with Story, Example, Analogy, and Testimony. Remembering that the human mind is a picture gallery, not just a debating chamber, we stand between the words of the text and the hearts of the people by communicating frequently at the bottom of the ladder of abstraction, using concrete support material. This means that you take a general truth such as "God values justice," or a vague exhortation such as "be good," and bring that down to *terra firma*, the world of your listeners.

To explain 1 Thessalonians 4:3 ("Avoid sexual immorality") we could state an abstract definition of the Greek term *porneia* ("a broad term that includes most forms of sexual promiscuity"), but we will also cite examples from current events, movies, or TV shows. When explaining, we move from the known to the unknown.

Take another example from 1 Thessalonians 4:8 ("Whoever disregards this teaching disregards God"). Your audience analysis might reveal that the congregation disagrees. They feel that their sexuality has nothing to do with their relationship to God. They love God, and they are sleeping around. So, to convince them that God really means what he says in verse 8, you might use an analogy of a play rehearsal. The director instructs an actor to move downstage, but the actor moves up-upstage. Time after time as the players run the scene, the actor keeps moving upstage. This leads to a rift between the actor and director because deliberately disregarding the director's instructions is a way of disregarding the director.

Other forms of support material also exist besides SEAT, such as quotations and statistics, but those forms work best when coupled with concrete forms such as SEAT. The human mind craves concrete images.

- Stories
  - Strengths and Weaknesses
    These are excellent at explaining, proving, and applying, but a single story can take three or more minutes. That time usually is well invested, but most sermons can afford only a few stories.

  - Example from James 4:13-17 ("Our days are short")
    Last year about this time Deacon Smith was meeting with his small group on a Wednesday night. The phone rang, and the voice on the other end of the receiver stammered in choked and broken words: "You son has been in an accident"... (Finish the story). We hardly need the reminder, yet the reminder comes to us in verse 15: We are as thin and as fragile as mist. Our days are short.

- Examples
  - Strengths and Weaknesses
    These are brief instances, miniature stories. They can be as short as a few words. Our sermons should bristle with examples. They are efficient, interesting, and relevant. They are a prime way to adapt the truth to your particular group of listeners, helping you stand between two words. The only

weakness with examples is that, being specific, they may not connect with some members of the audience. This can be overcome by using multiple examples. Somehow the human mind takes particulars and translates them into universals and then re-particularizes for personal identification.

- o Examples from James 4:13-17 ("Our days are short")

    - Daniel Boone made his own cherry wood coffin years before he died. He kept it under his bed, and when visitors came, he would pull it out and lie in it to show them how well it fit. This is how he reminded himself and others that our days are short.

    - Trappist monks always have an open grave on the grounds of their property. When one of their brothers dies, they put him in that grave, and then dig another. In this way, they constantly remind themselves that our days are short.

    - The smallest microbe, the most unlikely mechanical failure, or the least expected natural disaster is enough to convince us of the truth of verse 15—our days are short. Our lives are a vapor.

- Analogies
    - o Strength and Weaknesses
      Because effective communicators move from the known to the unknown, analogies help clarify new concepts. That is, an analogy turns on the hall light so that listeners will not stumble through a difficult verse. Analogy takes listeners by the hand and guides them through the maze. Analogies work best

when followed immediately by real or realistic examples. A drawback is that they can be hard to create. You have to have the skill and patience of a poet to ask: what is this like?

- Examples from John 4:13-17 ("Our days are short")

    - Job said, "My life is but a breath" (7:7).

    - Moses said we are like grass that springs up and then withers (Ps. 90)

    - Paul said we are like a flapping tent being dismantled by the wind (2 Cor. 5)

    - David said, "My days are a mere handbreadth," (Ps. 39:4-5).

- Testimony
    - Strength and Weaknesses
    People long to hear how other people respond to the truth, especially how they are applying it, or what keeps them from applying it. In particular, when done with humility and prudence, our listeners long to hear how the preacher is living the text.

    Using John Stott's model once again, the bridge between two worlds is the preacher. God has ordained that truth be incarnated, so we are not backward about revealing our own questions and reactions to the text. Just make sure that your self-disclosure illuminates the truth and the beauty of God. Don't turn the pulpit into the confessor's chamber or psychiatrist's couch.

    - Example from James 4:13-17 ("Our days are short")
    Last year about this time, as I was meeting with my small group on a Wednesday night, the phone rang.

> My brother informed me that ... (Finish the self-disclosure). I thought of the words of James 4: "What is your life? You are a mist." Our days are short.

Link the Points with Clear Transitions

Oral discourse occurs in time. It starts at, say 11:20 and ends at 11:49. It is a fluid river of words that, once spoken, pass on never to return. The words linger only until the echo fades. In contrast, written discourse occurs in space. You are reading this article on your computer screen, or perhaps you have printed it. You hold spatial objects—sheets of paper. With written discourse, the rate of communication is under the control of the receiver. You can read one sentence twice, ponder it, underline it, discuss it with the person next to you, skip it, or lay the sheets aside and return to them next week. You control the flow of information.

Not so in oral communication. The flow is under the control of the sender, not the receiver. Communication breakdown occurs frequently in oral communication because speakers forget that simple distinction. Those speakers state key concepts only once, as if they were writing, not speaking. They believe that once is sufficient, but in reality those key concepts are quickly engulfed in the current of words sweeping past the listener. Experienced speakers know that repetition and restatement are essential to avoid communication breakdown.

When we apply that axiom to the topic of this chapter—structure—we see that transitions are some of the key concepts that must be stated and restated. They help listeners stay up with our flow of thought. A good transition will feel labored and redundant to the speaker, but listeners will be grateful that you briefly freeze the river with deliberate redundancy, giving them time to catch up with the river of words. Most listeners have only a foggy sense of what we are talking about as we preach. Blessed is the man or woman who links points with clear, direct, fulsome transitions.

For example, imagine that you are done talking about the first point in your sermon from Psalm 32. You are twelve minutes into your sermon and are now ready to move into the second point. Being an experienced preacher, you know that the minds of your listeners have wandered in the last twelve minutes, so they need to be recollected. Unlike readers, who can review what they have read, and who have visual markers like paragraph indentions and headlines, the listeners have only your words and your delivery to help them move from one idea to the next. Knowing that if you state your transition only once, the listeners will not differentiate that sentence from the other sentences flowing across their ears in the river of words, you will freeze the river momentarily:

I. *Problem:* When we refuse to confess our sins, we bake in the oven of discipline. (vv. 3-4)

> *Transition: We have seen the problem: namely, when we refuse to confess, we experience the discipline of God. Now let's look at the solution, the way out of this dilemma. Rather than stubbornly refusing to confess, we come clean. We confess, we admit the truth about ourselves. When we mess up, we 'fess up. That is the solution to our problem. Verse 5 shows us that we should confess.*

II. *Solution:* Confess your sins. (vv. 5,1-2)

Notice some of the features of this transition: it *reviews* the previous point, uses synonyms for *purposeful redundancy*, and states bluntly the *logical relationship* of the points (problem-solution). To reiterate, such pedestrian transitions feel labored to the speaker, but listeners will rise up and call you blessed.

Write the Introduction and Conclusion

The purposes of the introduction are well known: gain attention, surface need, and introduce the sermon or the entire big idea. The preacher desires involuntary attention, so that listeners are riveted to the Word. The best way to achieve that is with a crisp opening statement that quickly "promises" that the sermon will address needs. Sur-Surface need, and you will have the attention you desire.

The preacher can use stories, current events, illustrations, anecdotes, rhetorical questions or comments in the introduction to focus the congregation's attention on the message to be preached. Since people often have distracted and wandering minds, a well-crafted introduction helps to arrest their attention by creating in them a desire to listen to what is being preached. Your introduction should be so engaging that if you only give that and drive home, your introduction should compel your audience to follow you home for the rest of the sermon. Provided here are some different kinds of introductions that might be used to secure people's attention.

1. *Current events*
   Current events that everyone knows about, or which may be interesting to them can be used to create interest and focus attention on what will be preached.

   Example: *Yesterday I was reading the Daily News and came across an article that said, "Many scientists believe man evolved 5 million years ago." How does this square with the Bible which says that man was created about six thousand years ago? Can you believe both? Well this morning we are going to see what the Word of God says and answer some of the common arguments evolutionists use to try and prove the earth is millions of years old and that man evolved from lesser life forms rather than being created by God.*

2. *Stories*
   Stories did not use at the beginning of a sermon nor talk are also very effective. People love stories and don't want to miss any part of them. Even short stories cause people to listen very carefully and focus their attention on the preacher or speaker. If the preacher can start off telling a story that relates to the text in some way, he will have everyone paying close attention. Consider these

lines and notice how they make you want to either complete them or find what they refer to:

a. Once upon a time...
b. There was a certain man...
c. The kingdom of heaven is like...
d. The other day...
e. Have you ever heard the story about...

3. *Rhetorical questions*
Rhetorical questions promote thought, focus attention, and make people think about what you are preaching. It makes people answer the question asked in their mind and if they don't know the answer it makes them want to know the answer.

Example: *Do you think you pray too much? Do you think God wants you to pray more? If you answered "Yes", what are you going to do about your insufficient prayer life?*

4. *Shockers*
<u>Shockers should not be used very often</u>. They are extreme illustrations, statements, or stories designed to shock people into paying attention. Shockers are sometimes necessary when speaking to a youth group at camp that has not had very much sleep for several days.

Example: *The President of the United States was just shot! (Pause) These were the words heard all over the world on November 22nd, 1963.*

5. *Appealing to the imagination*
Appealing to the imagination is also very helpful at the beginning of a sermon. You appeal to people's thoughts, experiences, and feelings by asking them to imagine, consider, or remind themselves of something they have or might be able to imagine experiencing.

> Example: *Imagine how painful it would be to put your finger in the flame of a candle for 15 seconds! Imagine how long it would seem to have your entire body thrown into a fiery furnace for 15 seconds. Imagine how terrible it would be to be thrown into molten lava, never to be pulled out, never dying, always alive and fully aware of all your senses, suffering the torments of burning pain for ever and ever. We will discover that hell is worse than that.*

The purposes of the conclusion are to summarize and drive home the big idea. These goals are often accomplished with techniques like a simple review, an epitomizing illustration, or a well-conceived prayer. However it is done, the conclusion wraps a ribbon around the entire message to demonstrate its unity and move the listeners toward a specific response. I find that most pastors do well with their introductions but are hit-or-miss with conclusions. This occurs because we run out of time and energy in preparation, or we ourselves do not fully understand the unity of the message and its implications for everyday life. While application should be made throughout the sermon, the conclusion should bring the application to a burning focus.

In the conclusion you want to summarize what you told them, to restate the main outline points, emphasizing application and implementation. A good conclusion will exhort people to obey the Word of God. It should force them to make a choice, either choose to obey or choose to disobey. What God is telling them to do from the text should be clearly laid before them. This is usually done by summarizing main points, emphasizing application and exhorting them to submit to and obey God.

Expository preaching involves "labour" and sweat, especially the wearying work of structure, but five sure strokes of the hammer on anvil can help us shape our sermons with clarity and relevance.

Chapter 8 Varieties of Expository Sermons

This chapter is devoted to explaining the several varieties of expository sermons:
- Doctrinal
- Ethical
- Inferential
- Biographical
- Propositional

The terms topical, textual, and expository describe the methods of constructing a sermon as related to the text; these latter terms described the kinds of subject matter with which the text deals. A sermon is "expository" because it expounds and is limited to a consecutive passage of Scripture, but its subject matter may be "doctrinal," "ethical," or "biographical," etc. These terms will be defined and explained in order that the reader may clearly perceive what the author means by them. When they are used by other writers, they may mean something different.

The *doctrinal expository sermon*

The aim of the doctrinal expository sermon is to expound the doctrinal teaching of a text, one in which the unity of the sermon is based upon related doctrines or related aspects of a single doctrine as the txt permits. Paul devotes most of the first part of all his epistles to doctrinal matters. When one preaches upon a text taken from the doctrinal part of an epistle, he nearly always will have as his aim to teach and enforce Bible doctrine, so, the sermon would be classified as "doctrinal."

But in this book the term "doctrinal" will be used only to describe sermons which point out, explain, and apply doctrines, not to describe sermons which have as their principle aim to prove a proposition. Such proof sermons will be called "propositional" even where the subject matter is doctrinal.

The following will illustrate the nature of a doctrinal expository sermon:

JUSTIFICATION
Romans 5:1-9

I. The Need of Justification
   a. Man is without strength—verse 6
   b. Man is sinner—verse 8

II. The Provision for Justification
   a. God's love—verse 8
   b. Christ's death—verse 6

III. The Appropriation of Justification—verses 1-2
   --by faith

IV. The Results of Justification
   a. Access to Grace—verse 2
   b. Peace with God—verse 1
   c. Salvation from Wrath—verse 9
   d. Victory in Tribulation—verse 3
   e. Development of Character—verses 3-5
      1. Patience to experience
      2. Experience to hope
      3. Hope to shamelessness

The above example is expository because it is taken entirely from one passage of Scripture; it is synthetic in its construction because the points are not arranged in the same order in which they occur in the text; and it is doctrinal because its aim is to explain and enforce the doctrine of justification. When one sees how easily modern day church members are used into false cults and persuaded to dabble with religious fads, one becomes convinced that there ought to be more doctrinal expository preaching from our pulpits.

The *ethical expository sermon*

The aim of the ethical expository sermon is to discover, explain and enforce rules of right Christian conduct. In the latter chapters of Paul's epistles and in some parts of the Gospels, the material pertains to the conduct of the believer's life. Sermons built upon texts dealing with the Christian's morals and behavior or related aspects of one ethical ideal.

Note the following examples:

PASTORAL HABITS
Romans 14:12-21

I. Personal Habits Are Accountable to God—verse 12
II. Personal Habits Are Not to be Judged by Men—verse 13
III. Personal Habits Must not Offend the Weak—verses 15,20,21
IV. Personal Habits Are subordinate to Kingdom Interests—verses 17,19

A CHRISTIAN'S RESPONSIBILITY AS A CITIZEN
Romans 13:1-10

I. Reading Civil Obedience—verses 1-5
   a. Implicit obedience—verse 2
   b. Fearless obedience—verses 3,4

II. Regarding Financial Obligations—verses 6-8
   a. To the State—verses 6-7
   b. To every Creditor—verse 8

III. Regarding Social Morals—verses 9-10
   a. In accordance with Bible ethics—verse 9
   b. In accordance with Love's law—verse 10

If there is a tendency for some preachers to neglect ethical preaching, let them notice that a large place is given in the New Testament to the regulation of Christian conduct. To neglect ethical preaching is to overlook much of the Holy Word. If the neglect is due to a fear that ethical sermons will be poorly received, that fear is unfounded. Ethics in a topical sermon might be made offensive, because it might be thought to be personal, but in an expository sermon suspicion of personal antagonism is very unlikely. In addition, the expository sermon which is fully based upon the Scripture has more weight of divine authority and is more likely to be effective.

The *inferential sermon*

The division of the inferential sermon is derived from inferences drawn from the fact and details of a narrative text. A narrative text is one which tells a story such as history or parable. In a story, text ideas or facts are not directly stated, but must be inferred from the conduct of the characters in the narrative, their conversations, and their success or failure. The inferences may be of a doctrinal or ethical nature, but the inference from a narrative text instead of by direct statement by the author of the Bible book. Inferences when they are carefully made are almost binding as direct statements and they are often more vivid to the hearer. Not the following illustrative examples.

"A YOUNG MAN'S RUN"
2 Kings 5:20-27

I. Sin Begins with Covetousness. Verse 26
II. Sin Leads to Other Sins. Verse 25
III. Sin cannot be Kept Secret. Verse 26
IV. Sin's Allurement is Deceptive. Verses 20, 27
V. Sin Receives Sure Punishment. Verse 27

Notice that none of these facts about sin are directly stated by the author of Second Kings but they are inferred from the details of the story and from the conversations between the characters in the story, such as Gehazi, Naaman, and Elisha. Nearly all expository preaching from texts in historical sections of the Bible will be treated by related inferences. Paul says about Israeli history (1 Cor. 10:11), "Now all these things happened unto them for examples." Therefore, we are given liberty to construct inferential sermons. Care must be taken, however, not to make hasty inferences which do not harmonize with the teaching of the Scriptures as a whole. Wild spiritualizing, likewise, must be avoided. Inferential sermons are sometimes called "observational."

The *biographical expository sermon*

It seems that nothing interests people more than stories about other people. News (or gossip, for that matter) about another is like honey to flies—it rarely fails to attract a crowd. When tirelessly researched and skillfully presented, an invitation to peer into the life and character of a biblical personage brings with it an unveiling of sin and motivation toward maturity. Biblical principles are not abstract only; they occur on the stage of living history displayed in biblical personification. Since this is true, biographical preaching is a powerful true-to-life instrument eagerly waiting to be used as an effective tool in an expositor's repertoire.

The biographical expository sermon concentrates on the successes or failures, the good or bad characteristics of Bible character. These are discovered, discussed, and presented for the hearer to imitate or avoid. Again the facts deduced may be doctrinal or ethical in nature but of the facts are drawn from an appraisal of a biography instead of being directly enjoined, the sermon will be called "biographical". Observe the following example from the biographical sketch of Cornelius in Acts, the tenth chapter.

> **"WHY GOD USED CORNELIUS"**
> Acts 10:1-8
>
> I. He was a Man of Character—verse 1-2
>   a. He was a strong man: Moral—though a soldier
>   b. He was a devout man
>   c. He was a generous man
>   d. He was an influential man—"with all his house"
>
> II. He was a Man of Prayer—verses 2, 3, & 4
>   a. He prayed always.
>   b. He prayed with faith.
>   c. He prayed with yieldedness.
>
> III. He was a Man of Action—verses 5-8
>   He immediately obeyed God.

Biographical sermons are quite effective, because the greatest interest next to self-interest is human interest. All of us are interested in the successes and even the failures of others. Biographical sermons are splendid for preaching to young people, for they can be made very vivid and dramatic. Care must be taken in the preparation of the biographical sermon that, it is not simply an array of facts about an ancient person which lacks application to real present day problems and conditions.

An *analogical expository sermon*

The divisions of an analogical expository sermon are related parts of an analogy. An analogy is a relation or likeness between two things or of one thing to another, consisting in the remembrance not of the things themselves, but of two or more attributes, circumstances or effects." Life is said to be analogous to a sea voyage, not because there is outward similarity between them, but because they have similar characteristics, such as a start, peaceful and turbulent experiences, a purpose, and an end. Note the following illustration.

> # "THE CHRISTIAN'S RACE OF LIFE"
> ## Hebrews 12:1-2
>
> I. The Spectators at the Race.
>   The martyrs of Ch. 11 those who have run before us.
>
> II. The Training for the Race.
>   Putting off the heavy garments of sin.
>
> III. The Gait of the Race.
>   Patient Striving
>
> IV. The Judge of the Race.
>   Jesus the Starter and Finisher
>
> V. The Reward for the Race.
>   Sharing with Christ His exaltation

The actual activities of a Christian life do not outwardly resemble the running of a race, but there are characteristics of each with resemble, such as: spectators, training, patient striving, a judge, and a reward. This type of sermon can be made very vivid and usually is easy to remember. There are many such analogies in the Bible, nearly all of which make excellent sermon texts. Analogical sermons are very good for children and young people.

The *propositional expository sermon*

Here the divisions of the sermon are the arguments in proof of a proposition. The New Testament writers who wrote to instruct and encourage members of an infant church in the midst of a hostile world devoted a considerable portion of their epistles and Gospel to argument against pagan and false Judaist teaching. Many of those same controversies are still raging today and many of the arguments are as valid today as they were when they first were written. Permanent results in preaching depend upon moving the will as such as upon moving the emotions. Therefore there is a large place for argument in the preaching of this day of science and reason. Not all argument is a large part of the human element in successful preaching.

For some purposes and to some audiences, the preacher can well make the whole sermon a proof of a clearly stated proposition. A sermon is not propositional just because it has a proposition (theme) or because it contains arguments, but it is propositional when all divisions are parts of the proof of a single proposition.

Example:

THE RESURRECTION OF CHRIST
1 Corinthians 15:3-23

Proposition: That Jesus Christ arose from the Dead.
I. There are Many Witnesses to the Fact.
   a. Peter
   b. The Twelve
   c. Five Hundred brethren at once
   d. Paul by Revelation

II. The Opposite Conclusion is Absurd.
   a. Preaching would be vain.
   b. Faith would be vain
   c. Holy Men would be false witnesses.
   d. Faithful believers would be deluded sinners.
   e. All the righteous dead would have perished

III. Christ's resurrection is a Theological Necessity
   a. There must be a second Adam to nullify the sin and death imputed through the transgression of the first Adam

---

A sermon without a skeleton is like a man without a backbone or like an edifice without a framework. But as a man must be more than bones and a building more than rafters, so must a sermon be more than skeleton. The sermon skeleton must be clothed with living flesh. There must an elaboration of the skeletal ideas which constitute the sermon divisions. There are six methods of elaboration which many homiletical writers recognize (see Appendix).

Expository Alternatives

To be truly biblical, preaching can and should be expository, even if it is thematic, theological, historical, or biographical. Expository sermons of these types must be thoroughly biblical, not only in their foundation but in their superstructure as well. The effectiveness of the messenger and the power of the message depend upon a close attention to the Word presented with grammatical, historical, literary, and contextual accuracy. For these special kinds of expository messages, certain guidelines must prevail, and many tools are available to assist the research process, but there are no shortcuts. The path to powerful preaching inevitably demands diligence in the Word.

Just as preaching that is verse-by-verse is not necessarily expository; so also preaching that is not verse-by-verse is not necessarily non-expository. It is granted that some topical approaches are not expository, but such need not be and certainly should not be the case. No book deals with topics that directly impact daily life more than the Bible. Thus, to be effective, all topical preaching and teaching, whether the topic is thematic, theological, historical, or biographical, must be consumed with expounding the Word.

Jesus expounded the Scriptures powerfully (Mark 1:22), but not always verse by verse. As an expositor, He sometimes spoke topically, using many different Old Testament Scriptures as the basis of His teaching. Sometimes He touched on a specific theme or aspect of theology while at other times he employed a historical event or character. Yet he always used the Word as the foundation and as the building blocks of His instruction. On the basis Jesus' example, it can be unequivocally asserted that all truly biblical preaching is also expository and not necessarily restricted to a verse-by-verse format. It can take alternative forms, too.

Topical preaching has many benefits. First, used at the end of one book study and before starting another, it provides variety. The change from one type of presentation to another often contributes freshness and causes increased attentiveness. Preaching on a theme or salient point of doctrine can give people a greater understanding of a particular subject, resulting in a greater impact on their lives.

Topical preaching has a venerable place in the history of the craft. Its legitimacy is seen in the validity of biblical and systematic theology. While this should not be the first choice of the pastor-teacher, every pastor will preach topically on occasion. . . . Because the topical sermon can be more relentlessly unitary, one discovers that any list of the ten sermons which have most decisively influenced world culture and society consists mostly if not entirely of topical sermons.

Second, restricting preaching solely to the verse-by-verse method without including any kind of didactic treatment of major biblical themes, doctrines, and ethical teachings is to make an unbiblical distinction between preaching and teaching, thereby withholding from a congregation essential perspectives on the Word.

Is there any reason why we should meet them week after week but leave them ignorant of doctrinal meaning? The gospel cannot be divided within itself assigning one to the pulpit, the other to the church school. To separate one from the other is to kill both.

Contrary to what is frequently thought (and apparently taught); topical preaching is not always the easiest. In many respects, it is the most difficult when done with correctness and accuracy. Consider these reasons.

1. The biblical text often used for topical homilies is merely a springboard for launching a selected topic and has no inherent relationship to the topic of the message. When this happens, the preacher draws from his own personal perspectives, ideas, principles, and world view to develop the subject. This is not expository preaching. The preacher's proper task is to deliver the goods, not to manufacture them. He is the waiter, not the

chef. Therefore, the biblical text must be his resource, the fountain of truth to which he constantly resorts, from which he himself continually drinks, and from which he faithfully draws to satisfy the thirst of others. Exercising this kind of control over topical preaching is hard work.

2. The Scriptures garnered to support the emphasis of a topical message are many times wrested from their context, forcing them to teach something they do not. The memorization of selected verses of the Bible, beneficial in and of itself, frequently exacerbates the problem. For example, how often has Matt 18:20 been employed to console the faithful few at poorly attended prayer meetings rather than to assure divine presence and enablement in implementing church discipline? This type of pitfall is most common, often capturing its victims unwittingly. Avoiding this type of danger is very time-demanding. Whether the subject is thematic or theological, each Scripture must be thoroughly researched so as to do justice to his historical and literary context.

3. Though "problem preaching" or "life-situation preaching" may bring much contemporaneity to the pulpit and thus capitalize on relevant issues, it often generates greater focus on the problem than on the solution. It may also occasionally expose the preacher to a "he's-preaching-at-me" accusation.

Subject preaching is the creator's method par excellence. It lends itself to finished discourse. But it has its dangers. The preacher easily becomes interested in finding subjects that are interesting and readily yield a good oration rather than such as have a sure Christian and scriptural basis or such s come close home to the needs of his people. He is tempted to think more of his ideas and his sermons than of "rightly dividing the word of truth" and leading men into the Kingdom of God. He is in danger also of preaching in too narrow a field of truth and human need, since of necessity he will be drawn to those subjects that interest him personally or with which he is already familiar.

Unless, therefore, he is constantly widening his horizon by diligent study, he will soon exhaust his resources.

Consequently, great diligence is required to avoid a "problem only" orientation when using this method. With a reasonably broad coverage of the Bible in one's preaching a wide variety of problems and life situations can be addressed naturally and delicately without violating expository boundaries in employing a "topical" approach.

When preaching on a theme, a theological doctrine, or a historical event or character, the expositor must endeavor to utilize Scripture fully in his preaching. His task is to unfold the Scriptures, not merely to enfold them into a topic. The latter will bend the Word to conform to the preacher's perspective; the former will bend the preacher's perspective to conform to the Word. This is important, because it is that Word that is "living and active and sharper than any two-edged sword" (Heb 4:12). It is the Scriptures that bear witness about Christ (John 5:39). It is the Gospel that is "The power of God for salvation" (Rom 1:16). Desire to be relevant or current must not prevail over biblical authority.

Whether preaching thematically, theologically, historically, or biographically, the bottom line is that the Scriptures must be the primary resource and contextual guidelines must be observed. They are the expositor's chief source of spiritual insight and teaching, the place to which he turns first before studying the many available helps. And once in the Scriptures, the expositor must take great pains to utilize them in a fashion that will reflect the authorial intent.

Chapter 9. Expository Context

Contextualization and the Expository Sermon

At this point it becomes necessary to approach the question of value. What will be gained by making this distinction between expository hermeneutics and expository style of delivery? Since the expository method in both aspects has served the church well for many years, is it possible to lose more than is gained by trying to divide the procedure from the product? The answer lies in the matter of how the process of communication works. The ultimate purpose of communication includes reception by a listener or audience. If our style of preaching makes it hard for our audience to understand the message, then the importance of the message seems to demand that we look for a style which will communicate more effectively.

The linear, western-style logic of the expository preaching style has indeed served the western church well for many wears. But it is not possible to retain a faithful exegetical approach to Scripture while at the same time contextualizing our style of preaching so that the exposition of the text can be communicated cross-culturally in a style which will be more effective among non-western thinkers? Is it not possible that, with the encroachment of post-modernism on the western mind, even American preachers may have to consider the possibility that linear logic may very soon not be the best way of communicating with their own congregations? George Swank encourages preachers to at least take notice that today's congregation only leaves its TV sets briefly to hear a sermon and will not have the patience to follow extended logical discourse.

Missionary strategists have long noted that "organization is largely a matter of cultural preference." John T. Seamands says the missionary evangelist needs to develop an indigenous style of preaching that will fit the background and life-style of his audience. In the book <u>Communicating Christ Cross-Culturally</u>, the writer depicts a Japanese audience "if the speaker has good ethos and is a recognized authority, specific proofs and support are not needed." Donn Ketcham suggests that "many cultures are not given much to thinking in the abstract, but respond to the sort of teaching that conjures up in their minds mental pictures that are easily remembered.

Surely a Book replete with stories and narratives could be communicated to such people in a style which most effectively matches their cultural traditions. Tim Matheny suggests that certain portions of Scripture might even fit one culture better than another. According to Tim Matheny "the frequent use of poetic passages in the Old Testament usually does not impress the Westerner nearly as much as they do the Arab, whose life is filled poetic expressions." Likewise a culture which has a history of Christian influence should be able to use life stories from its own history rather than illustrating messages from the culture of the American missionary. It is important to make a conscious effort to incorporate the life and stories of Korean figures as much as possible into Korean preaching so that it becomes truly indigenous and accountable to the Korean cultural context.

Word choice is also very closely tied to cultural tastes. Not only must the communicator learn the language spoken by the audience in terms of French, or Spanish, or Arabic. The communicator must also learn the language choices acceptable to sub-cultures within those language groups. Randall Speirs gives an illustration of the lack of such adaptation among the Native Americans from Mexico.

> In Mexico, for example, some Indian preachers use Spanish even though they can barely get along in it. They do this despite the fact that a large part of their congregation, particularly the women, understands nothing of what they say. This strange behavior is brought about by the wrong kind of pride. Spanish is the language of prestige, and the preacher wants everyone to appreciate his ability to speak it.

Speakers of English, if honest, would admit that there are also times when pride of the same kind affects the ability to communicate with an audience. The speaker either has not taken the time to analyze his audience, or he has learned a theological language which holds great meaning for him but is not translated into the language of those to whom he is preaching.

Warren Stewart discusses the experience of black preachers who in recent years have had the opportunity to attend college and seminary. "With the exposure to theological institutions of higher learning has come the necessity to learn and acquire another language uncommon in form (but not in substance) with the language of those to whom most of their preaching will be directed. The language to which I have reference is the primarily cerebral and abstract vernacular of white Anglo-Saxon Protestant theologians and biblical scholars." Once this new language is acquired Stewart argues that "the truth that needs to be conveyed through the Word must be posited before the people in an understandable tongue." Word choice as well as organization must communicate with the target audience. Attention to capturing the exact meaning of the words from the original languages will not be of benefit to the listener unless the preacher goes through the process of phrasing those ideas in words which carry meaning for them.

The growth of missions work among those of Jewish heritage has likewise required some careful and culturally sensitive word choices. Among some of the congregations of those who prefer being called Messianic Jews "the Anglicized word *Christ* is dropped in favor of *Messiah*." Although a western audience might be uncomfortable dropping the familiar word *Christ* from its worship experience, using *Messiah* certainly communicates the same concept.

This process of interpreting the text for the audience is really the essence of the homiletical task. Kevin J. Vanhoozen writes "We appropriate the meaning of a text when we let its world into ours, when we put its pages into our practice." If a sermon faithfully explains the text so that the audience understands the biblical revelation of God and His will, that sermon can be called expository even if it does not fit the strictures of expository preaching as a method of organization. In fact, for that audience it may be far more effective in expositing the Word. Walter Liefeld implies this distinction when he writes, "The essential nature of expository preaching, then, is preaching that explains a passage in such a way as to lead the congregation to a true and practical application of that passage."

Preaching cross-culturally then could conceivably be accomplished through story-telling, inductive argument, debate, drama, generalization, specific examples, narrative preaching, or any number of other styles while at the same time maintaining absolute fidelity to the exposition of the text. "The missionary mandate is to make the Bible clearly understood and to help the national apply the Word of God in his own situation in his own culture." William Thompson suggests a model by which such a sermon could be shaped.

> Any model we might produce would certainly have to utilize the techniques of exegesis and the principles of interpretation. It would have to provide for an honest engagement with the biblical text and an equally honest faceting of life as the listeners are living it out. A model would have to take seriously the theological dimensions of the material at hand, placing the gospel—the work of God—at its center, but taking into account the doctrine of sin and also the ethical consequences of the gospel.
>
> The model ought also to recognize and utilize the dynamic of biblical story, the encounters of people and ideas. It ought to facilitate the formulation of a central idea that will control the selection and arrangement of the sermonic material, but it should not, however, be primarily a homiletical model that might make all the sermons it produces sound alike; it should engender variety rather than uniformity.

Such a model would remain faithful to the spirit of the expository hermeneutic if it incorporated the characteristics which Liefeld says are present in every true expository message. These are characteristics which depend on our approach to the text and not our approach to organization. They include a method which "deals with one passage of Scripture" (while allowing for a topical method which draws its essential information from the text), "hermeneutical integrity," "cohesion," "movement and direction," and "application."

All of those characteristics can be present in styles of preaching which adapt to a variety of cross-cultural audiences. "The message is totally from God, but its form is culturally conditioned."

Implications of the Contextualization of Expository Preaching

Acceptance of the distinction between expository preparation and expository preaching as a style will care some implications for preachers in whatever culture they serve, as well as for schools who seek to train men in homiletics. The first of these implications will be presented in the context of warnings.

While seeking to distinguish between expository content and expository form, a preacher must heed the warning of William Willimon not to lose the message while seeking to contextualize the form the message takes.

> I see here (in Acts 17) an invitation and a warning to preachers who want to contextualize the gospel. The invitation is to start where the people are, but the warning is to recognize our limited ability to adapt the gospel. Eventually the gospel is about something for which there is no precedent—the resurrection—and we can only testify to it. The truth claims of Christianity are not easily validated externally. They're a matter of faith.

This warning is echoed by John Stott, who says the preacher must avoid two opposite errors in the process of sermon preparation. "The first is belief that though it was heard in ancient times, God's voice is silent today. The second is the claim that God is indeed speaking today, but that His Word has little or nothing to do with Scripture." While trying to contextualize the form of preaching in order to adapt to an audience, the preacher must always heed the warning not give up the message of Scripture which has been discovered through historical-grammatical exegesis.

The second warning involves the matter in which sermon preparation takes place. There is a danger when using other forms of preaching than the one commonly called expository that the emphasis will jump from the research of the text to the needs of the audience. The preacher will begin with the application and neglect the disciplined study which should be present before adaptation and application. Calvin Miller says, "Precept preachers are, by their very nature, more given to consistent spiritual disciplines (and for that matter, discipline of any sort) than story-oriented preachers." The preacher who desires to use story must be warned against neglecting the discipline of ardent study.

The other implications for preachers and those who train them will involve some questions communicators must face.

1. Am I open to learning from other cultures or have I concluded that the methods I use are the only legitimate way to preach? D.A. Carson says "Genuine exchanges and mutual correction among leaders who hold a high view of Scripture but who work and labor in highly diverse contexts should prove enriching to the entire church of God."
2. What kind of preaching should we expect from our missionaries when they return from the field if they have been ardently working to contextualize their communication?
3. Should our training in the area of homiletics, especially in academic institutions we start in other countries, include the possibility that expository content may need to be communicated in some other for than an expository organization depending on the target audience and culture of the potential listeners?
4. Is it possible that continued influence of post-modernism will bring the American preacher to the place where he must explore the possibility of using other styles of preaching to communicate to an audience which is no longer able to follow linear, logical reasoning?

These questions must be answered in light of the fact that Scripture holds the preacher to textual faithfulness but does not limit him to any particular style or form of communication. They must be answered if we can legitimately distinguish between expository content and expository organization.

Mandate of Biblical Inerrancy

The theological highlight of recent years has without question been intense focus on biblical inerrancy. Much of what has been written defending inerrancy represents the most acute theological reasoning our generation has produced. Yet it seems our commitment to inerrancy is somewhat lacking in the way it fleshes out in practical ministry. Specifically, preaching ought to reflect our conviction that God's Word is infallible and inerrant. Too often it does not. In fact, there is a discernable trend in contemporary Christianity away from biblical preaching and a drift toward an experience-center, pragmatic, topical approach in the pulpit.

Should not our preaching be biblical exposition, reflecting our conviction that the Bible is the inspired, inerrant Word of God? If we believe that "all Scripture is inspired by God" and inerrant, must we not be equally committed to the reality that it is "profitable for teaching, for reproof, for correction, for training in righteousness; that the man of God may be adequate, equipped for every good work" (2 Tim 3:16-17)? Should not that magnificent truth determine how we preach?

Any form of preaching that ignores the intended purpose and design of God falls short of the divine plan. Preaching appears in the Bible as a relaying of what God has said about Himself and His doings, and about men in relation to Him, plus a pressing of His commands, promises, warnings, and assurances, with a view to winning the hearer or hearers to a positive response.

The only logical response to inerrant Scripture, then, is to preach it in such a way that the meaning of the Bible passage is presented entirely and exactly as it was intended by God. Expository preaching is the proclamation of the truth of God as mediated through the preacher.

Admittedly, not all expositors have an inerrant view; neither does all with an inerrant view practice expository preaching. These are, however, inconsistencies because an inerrantist perspective demands expository preaching and a non-inerrantist perspective make it unnecessary.

It is no secret that Christ's Church is not at all in good health in many places of the world. She has been languishing because she has been fed, as the current line has it, "junk food", all kinds of artificial preservatives and all sorts of unnatural substitutes have been served up to her. As a result, theological and Biblical malnutrition has afflicted the very generation that has taken such giant steps to make sure its physical health is not damaged by using foods or products that are carcinogenic or otherwise harmful to their physical bodies. Simultaneously a worldwide spiritual famine resulting from the absence of any genuine publication of the Word of God (Amos 8:11) continues to run wild and almost unabated in most quarters of the Church.

The cure is expository preaching.

The mandate is clear. Expository preaching is the declarative genre in which inerrancy finds its logical expression and the church has its life and power. Stated simply, inerrancy demands exposition as the only method of preaching that preserves the purity of Scripture and accomplishes the purpose for which God gave us His Word. The principle that Christian preaching is proclamation of the Word must obviously be determinative of the content of the sermon.

G. Campbell Morgan, hailed as the twentieth century's "prince of expositors," was a messenger widely used by God. There was a time in his life, however, when he wrestled with the very issue we discuss. He concluded that if there were errors in the biblical message, it could not be honestly proclaimed in public.

Chapter 10 Effective Delivery

Theological sermons need not be dry. Broadus observes that it "all depends on the way in which it is done. The dry preacher will make all subjects dry; dull anecdotes and tame exhortations have sometimes been heard of. Conversely, theological sermons can and should be as fresh and vibrant as the pastor's own zeal for knowing God, his zest for discovering the deep riches of God's Word, and his passion for preaching the whole counsel of God. Much more than a theological lecture is required; mandated is a treatise passionately delivered and overflowing with evidence that the subject has captured the heart and life of the pastor and now begs to infiltrate the innermost being of the hearer.

The human voice is one of the most precious gifts that God has given to mankind. Through the voice we are able to express how we feel, what we have seen, what have accomplished and what knowledge we hold in our minds. God also ask us to use the gift of speech to tell others about His great plan of salvation. God says, "Go ye therefore, and preach..." Preaching is performed primarily through the utilization of our voices. We may have knowledge, but unless we know how to use the voice correctly, our work will be a failure... Knowledge will be of little advantage to us unless we cultivate the talent of speech.

Jesus as Orator

I do not believe that anyone reading this book will disagree with me when I say that Jesus was the world's greatest living orator. I say this on the premise of the Scriptures where we see that people recognized Jesus as a great speaker because He was different from the other preachers of His time (John 7:46). His authority came from God. He spoke clearly (*enunciated*) and in an interesting way (Matt 7:28-29).

The author of Desire of Ages also described his language was pure, refined and clear as a running stream. Jesus' voice was music to the ears of those who had been accustomed to the monotonous, spiritless preaching of the scribes and Pharisees. He spoke slowly and impressively, emphasizing those words to which He wished His hearers to give special heed.

Study carefully the methods Jesus used to teach His hearers eternal truths. Notice and copy how He held their interest.
- His preaching was preceded by prayer (Luke 5:16)
- His preaching was based on Scripture
- He used many illustrations from nature
- He used simple parables to teach important truths
- His preaching was aimed at meeting the needs of the people
- He visited and talked with all kinds of people. This helped Him to understand what to preach about.

Church Leaders as Public Speakers

It is extremely important for church leaders to know how to prepare interesting material and how to present that material in an interesting way. However, it is even more important for them to learn how to speak clearly so that they can present their carefully prepared material in words that can be heard and understood. Any church leader who neglects the development of his voice is doing discredit to the cause of God. (Titus 2:8; Nehemiah 8:8)

Ministers of the gospel should know how to speak with power and expression, making the words of eternal life so expressive and impressive that the hearers cannot but feel their weight. I am pained when I hear the defective voices of many of our ministers. Such ministers rob God of the glory He might have if they trained themselves to speak the word power ... if he attempts to speak to the people without knowing how to use the talent of speech, half his influence is lost, for he has little power to hold the attention of the congregation.

Preachers are called to be ministers of the word of God. This means that the sermon should be much more than one man's opinion; the sermon should be the word of God. A sermon is the word of God only to the extent that it faithfully proclaims the word of God in the Bible. The Word of God rightly divided brings authority to the sermon, thereby protecting the preacher from heresy and, at the same time, giving the audience a means to validate and defend the instruction.

The culture and right use of the voice are greatly neglected ... there are many who read and speak in so low or so rapid a manner that they cannot be readily understood. Some have a thick indistinct utterance, others speak in a high key, in sharp, shrill tones that are painful to the hearers ... This is an evil that can and should be corrected ... By diligent effort all may acquire the power to read intelligibly, and speak in a full, clear, round tone, in a distinct and impressive manner. By doing this we may greatly increase our efficiency as workers for Christ.

Developing Your Speaking Voice

I. How sounds and speech are made?
 The sounds that come from our mouths as words are produced by three different actions.

    1. Abdominal, Diaphragm and Chest Muscles.
 The diaphragm is a large muscle that stretches across the bottom of our rib-cage between our lungs and our stomach. The diaphragm is an important muscle in the production of sound. When it moves upwards, it pushes air from the lungs forcing it out through the vocal cords.
 The abdominal muscles are also very important for good speaking. These muscles in concert with the chest muscles assist the diaphragm to push air out of the lungs. By learning to control both the abdominal muscles and the diaphragm, a good speaker will be able to speak powerfully without his throat becoming sore.

    2. Vocal Cords.
 Vocal cords are very thin pieces of skin-like material stretched across the voice-box in our throats. When air from our lungs passes over them they vibrate and make a noise.

3. Tongue, Mouth and Nasal Passages.
   The sounds that are made by the vocal cords are turned into words by the movement of the tongue and lips. The quality of the words and their tone are produced as the sound passes through the mouth and nasal passages.

For good speech to be produced, the vocal cords, the diaphragm, abdominal muscles, chest muscles, tongue, mouth and nasal passages must all be used.

II. Correct Breathing
   Many speakers do not breathe correctly. Their breathing is far too shallow and they only use half of their lung space. When a person breathes in, his whole chest should fill with air. The diaphragm should move down drawing in the air. The abdominal muscles will relax and be seen to move out a little. When a person breathes out, the abdominal muscles will tighten and the diaphragm will move upwards forcing out the air.

   When a person is speaking in public, he must think about his breathing. If he is breathing correctly, using the diaphragm muscle to pull air in and out to force air out, then he will be able to speak forcefully. If he only takes in shallow breaths, then his throat will soon get sore from talking because it is not getting any help from his abdominal muscles and diaphragm.

   Breathing Exercises Lie with your back on a flat surface i.e. bed, floor etc. Place a heavy object on your abdomen. A large book will do. Now breathe in deeply and hold your breath. Did the book on your abdomen rise? If you breathed in deeply, the book should have been raised two or three inches by your abdomen. Next, breathe out. Push the air out with your diaphragm muscles. Watch the book on your abdomen go down. Force all the air out. Practice this exercise for five minutes every day until you are breathing correctly and naturally.

Develop your diaphragm muscle by standing up straight and breathing in and out quickly like a dog that has just been running fast. Force the air in and out with your diaphragm. Ha a ha a ha a ha a ha etc. Feel your diaphragm muscle working. You should be able to feel it getting a little bit sore. Stop the exercise. Try it again. Do this every day also. It will develop this muscle and give your voice more power when you speak.

> To ensure correct delivery in reading and speaking, see that the abdominal muscles have full play in breathing and that the respiratory organs have unrestricted. Let the strain come on the muscles of the abdomen, rather than on those of the throat. Great weariness and serious disease of the throat and lungs may thus be prevented.

III. Clarity of Speech

Many speakers have lazy mouths. Their tongues do not move enough to pronounce each word clearly. Their mouths do not open wide enough to let the words come out clearly. Often they speak far too quickly and their words get cut off and tumble out of their mouths all mixed up. Unless you speak clearly and slowly, your listeners will soon grow tired of hearing you and the importance of your message will be lost.

> By earnest effort we are to obtain a fitness for speaking. This fitness includes uttering every syllable clearly, placing the force and the emphasis where they belong. Speak slowly. Many speak rapidly, hurrying one word after another so fast that the effect of what they say is lost.

Speaking Exercises Say the following sounds to practice opening your mouth wide. "Ba a, da a, la a, ma a, ta a." Say them over again. Open your mouth. Push the sound out with your diaphragm muscle. Practice this exercise often.

The following exercise will help you use your tongue to speak each word clearly. Put your first two fingers together. Now put the end of your two fingers between your front teeth. Now while you are holding your teeth gently on your fingers say your ABCs. Move your tongue around to carefully form each of the letters. When you have finished this exercise, take your Bible and start reading aloud from it. As you read each word, pronounce each word clearly and distinctly. Speak slowly enough to say each word clearly. Every day, practice reading out loud in this way. Listen to yourself and make sure that each word is sounded clearly.

One final exercise is to record yourself speaking or preaching on a voice recorder. Play back the recording and listen to yourself. This will help you to hear yourself as others hear you. Try to correct the mistakes you hear yourself making.

IV.   Use Good Language
As good leaders, we are often called on to preach and speak for God. Let us speak God's word correctly. Watch that no bad language or impure speech comes from our lips. Do not use expressions of speech that will offend your listeners. Do not be crude or rude in your speech or in your illustrations. Whatever language you are preaching in, use the correct language and the right words.

> "The workman for God should make earnest efforts to become a representative of Christ, discarding all uncomely gestures and uncouth speech. He should endeavor to use correct language." (Counsels to Teachers)

1 Corinthians 1:21 "... it please God by the foolishness of preaching to save them that believe."

Many in the world may consider that preaching is foolishness. However, preaching is God's way of using people to reach others with His message of salvation. If God has chosen preaching as His way, let us do all we can to improve our speaking voices so that we will be fit channels for God to work through.

How to Preach a Sermon
1. Be Prepared to Preach
    a. Be spiritually prepared. Feel God's touch in your life. (1 Samuel 10:26)
        i. Make right:
            - Known sins that have not been confessed
            - Dishonest practices
            - Careless speech
            - Refusal to follow God's commands
            - Unresolved disagreement with other people

        ii. The preacher should:
            - Spend time every day in Bible study and prayer
            - Have earnest desire to overcome sin
            - Be careful to follow God's standards of behavior both in public and in private
            - Live at peace with others.

    b. When we enter the pulpit, there must be a fire in our hearts (Luke 24:32)
        i. That fire comes from:
            - A heart made right with God
            - The conviction that our message comes from God
            - The assurance of the Holy Spirit
            - The confidence of knowing our topic well

2. Speak Correctly
Because the voice is very important in preaching, we should be very careful to use it in the best way possible. Take care of the following things:

a. Volume
Always speak loud enough so that all may hear you. However, do not shout for you will offend people. Do not speak too quietly tor people will not hear you. The easiest speaking voice to listen is the one that varies with volume. You may speak loudly at times and sometimes you may speak quietly. Change the volume to fit what you are saying. Use your diaphragm muscle to change your volume.

b. Tone and Pitch
Someone who speaks through their nose or in a high pitched, squeaky voice is very hard to listen to. Practice speaking in your own house. Practice so that your voice comes out round and full. Listen to yourself on a tape recorder. Push from your diaphragm and open your mouth so that the sound will come out clearly.

c. Speak Clearly
Many speakers have lazy tongues. Form each word carefully and speak it clearly. Open your mouth and let the words come out. Do not mumble with your mouth half closed. If you do not speak clearly, God's truth will not be clearly understood. You should practice to pronounce each word correctly and distinctly.

d. Speak Slowly
Often, carefully prepared sermons are not understood by the listeners because the preacher speaks to quickly. Slow down your speaking so that you can clearly pronounce each word. This will help your listeners to understand what you saying. Listen to yourself on the recorder. Ask your wife or friend to tell you if you are speaking took quickly. Then practice speaking more slowly.

3. Speak Positively
    a. Be positive, do not express doubts in the pulpit
    b. Be truthful and accurate in all that you say

c. Be respectful of the feelings and opinions of others. Never condemn or speak disrespectfully of another person or church
d. Be humble. Do not give the impression that you know everything.
e. Be earnest. Preach to the hearts of the people. Preach for decisions for Jesus
f. Uplift Jesus, not yourself (John 12:32; John 3:30)

4. Hold the Attention of Your Hearers
   a. Look your listeners in the eye. Do not stare out the window or at the ceiling as you talk. Let your eyes move around to each of the listeners. Let them know that you are talking to them.
   b. Smile as you preach. Be careful not to look angry. Do not condemn or speak harshly to your listeners. This will make it much easier for them to accept your sermon.
   c. Ask questions. Make them think. By their answers you will know whether or not they understand what you are saying.
   d. Ask them to open their Bibles and turn to the texts. Ask church members to help those who are having trouble finding the text. Involve them in the Scripture readings.
   e. Show them pictures that illustrate your point.
   f. Hold up objects; for example, a stone, lamp, knife
   g. Act out character in your sermon; for example, Zacchaeus - bend down to show how short he was
   h. Have the children guess who you are describing
   i. Use hand gestures
   j. Speak like you imagine the person in your story might have spoken.

5. Use Illustrations and Stories
   Perhaps the best way to hold the interest of your listeners is to tell stories. Stories are like windows in a horse. They let in light and fresh air. Most people can concentrate on something for about ten to fifteen minutes. Then they lose interest. If you plan to call a story or use an illustration every ten minutes during your sermon,

then you will hold your listener's attention and interest right to the end of the sermon.

    a. Illustrations and Stories Come From
        i. Bible
        ii. Books, newspapers
        iii. Traditional stories
        iv. Other preachers
        v. People's life
        vi. Incidents that take place around us everyday

    b. Different types of stories and Illustrations
        i. Personal experiences
        ii. Bible stories
        iii. Parables
        iv. Poems
        v. Current events

6. Use the Blackboard

By using the blackboard, your message will enter the minds of your listeners through their eyes as well as their ears. The action of writing on the backboard will capture their interest.

On the blackboard you can:
    a. Write words
    b. List Bible texts
    c. List your main points
    d. Draw pictures and charts

Even though you may not be able to write neatly or draw well, still use the blackboard. Whatever you write or draw will strengthen what you have said in your listener's thinking.

7. Develop your Theme Logically
Your sermon should contain three points
    a. Introduction – Capture the attention of the congregation and prepare them for what you are going to talk about.

b. Main Body - Develop the theme. You will take the congregation step-by-step from one point to the next, helping them to understand the truth you are presenting.

c. Conclusion - Summarize quickly the main points of your sermon. The conclusion will include some device (question, story, text etc.) to help each listener make a decision for Christ.

As you preach, develop your theme. Make your point, and then carefully explain it. Be alert to the reactions of your listeners. Ask them if what you have said is clear. Then move on to your next point. State each main point clearly. Repeat your main points in different ways so that your listeners will understand where you are heading in your talk. Part way through your sermon; summarize the main events you have already covered. Move step-by-step through the sermon joining together you main points.

8. Read Bible Verses Carefully
   Often the power of God's word is lost by poor reading. While reading the Bible, many preachers stumble over some words and pronounce others incorrectly. Practice reading the Bible texts while preparing your sermon. Read them out loud using the right expression and pronunciation. In the pulpit, do you look down as you read? Hold the Bible up in your hands and read clearly. You are handling God's word. Read it carefully and correctly.

John 12:21. As we stand up to preach, the people listening are saying to us, "Sir, we would see Jesus." Let us not disappoint them. Let us uphold the Master before them that were main experience his saving grace in their lives.

Three Delivery Methods

This author recognizes three distinctive methods for delivering the Word of God and they are:

A. **Preaching with no notes** is recommended by those who feel that spontaneity and eye contact are of the utmost importance. In fact some people think it is important not to use notes so that you don't quench the "unction of the Holy Spirit."

Preaching with no notes does have its advantages. You are able to maintain almost constant eye contact. Your speech is often more natural, which usually means more engaging, and less stilted and formal. You don't have to stick close to a pulpit to read your notes which allows you to wander around and speak directly at people. Preaching with no notes creates a more natural and less artificial sermon delivery.

The downside of preaching with no notes is that you have to remember everything you are going to say, virtually memorizing your sermon. Either that or you just wing it and see what comes to mind from what you have studied. People who preach with notes often have a hard time keeping the length of their sermon under control. They often end up rushing to finish because they have spent too much time explaining things earlier on.

For those with great minds and the gift of gab, they are able to do a pretty good job with no notes. But usually a person with no notes is never as precise and concise as a person with notes. Usually the person with no notes ends up repeating himself and leaving out important detail. Yet, if you are gifted and able to preach with no notes and still maintain accuracy, detail, depth, and conciseness, there is nothing wrong with it.

B. **Preaching with an outline** is practiced by many preachers. These kinds of preachers come in many varieties. Some like to go into the pulpit with a single 3"x5" card with their outline on side and a few notes on the back to help jog their memory about key details or illustrations. Others have a very detailed outline with their sub-points, notations, quotes, illustrations, and applications all written out.

The advantages of having an outline are that it helps you be precise, concise, and accurate. You can include key word definitions, quotes, and cross references without having to memo-memorize them or leave them out altogether. Since you don't have a manuscript, you still are able to maintain good eye contact with your congregation.

The problem with preaching with just an outline or detailed outline is that you lose much of the fruit of your study. Three months later you can't remember very much of what you studied. If you had to preach the same sermon several years later, using the same detailed outline, you would pretty much have to study the entire text completely from scratch.

Some have tried to compensate for this by first typing out a complete manuscript and then creating an outline from it to take into the pulpit. This allows the preacher to both record all the fruits of his study and yet still have the advantages of a detailed outline in the pulpit. Yet creating both a manuscript and a detailed outline is more labor intensive.

C. **Preaching with full notes or a manuscript** is also very common. The preacher prepares an entire manuscript and writes down pretty much everything he is going to say. The good part about having a full manuscript is that you have a complete record of your studies and if asked to preach the same sermon again, you can read over your manuscript several times, make some minor changes, update some illustrations and preach it again with much less effort.

You can also merge sermon manuscripts together and convert them into prose suited for books, journals, and magazine articles. Not only that, if you are working on a Bible study or writing a paper, you can copy and paste parts of various sermons into a document or study. And of course when you preach from a full manuscript you are able to maintain precision in delivery, give important technical detail, maintain an even progression of thought and gauge the length of your sermon with certainty.

Disadvantages of using a manuscript are that the preacher can become slave to his own notes, always looking down and reading, rather than making eye contact with his people. The preacher, who preaches from full notes and doesn't read well, often stumbles and seems less fluid and more stilted. He gives his people the idea that they could read this better themselves.

The argument that preaching with notes "quenches the Holy Spirit" is just not true. Most of the greatest preachers who have ever lived preached from a manuscript. Besides the Holy Spirit can work through you while preparing your manuscript just as well as He can while preaching.

But these weaknesses can be overcome if the preacher learns to summarize portions of his notes rather than read them word for word. This way he can be more fluid and spontaneous, but still maintain good structure and accuracy, timing, and progression of thought.

Chapter 11 Sermon Do's and Don'ts

These are just some personal guidelines, observations and suggestions for the individual preparing for public ministry and preaching:

1. Don't preface any scripture reading with "...you've probably heard this before...' or '...you're probably quite familiar with this scripture....". Instead, read your scriptures boldly and without excuse. You thought it was important enough to include—then it must be important enough to read confidently. Don't give the congregation a reason to tune you out.

2. Don't tell stories and then just throw in a scripture to 'make it seem like a sermon.' Instead, let your scriptures be the basis of your message—let your stories have the purpose make your scriptures and spiritual lessons come to life.

3. The greatest of all scripture teachers use metaphors and analogies—you do the same. When God created us in his image—he divided our brains into two parts—right and left. The right side possesses the emotions, arts, feelings, etc.; the left, our reasoning skills, logic, etc. Jesus knew that effective teaching speaks to BOTH sides of a person's brain—the feelings and the logic. He never taught a principle (housed in the left side) without relating it to a situation in life that people had felt and experienced (right side). Engage the right brain/left brain when you speak, that is speak to the logical and emotional sides of people's brains. When both halves 'understand' the message, true learning occurs.

4. Teach from God's word. It is your primary responsibility. Choose the more difficult task of changing the culture to conform to God rather than transforming God's word to fit the culture. Don't be afraid to teach.

5. While it may seem personally significant to you, don't spend the first ten minutes telling how really weren't sure what you were going to talk about. Instead, introduce your talk with a spirit-catching introduction, and get down to business. (That is, start telling what it is you came to tell). Like the old saying goes '...you had to be there...' If the congregation wasn't 'there,' little spiritual value exists in rehearsing this.

6. Never, ever, EVER say I really didn't want to be here today.' Oh sure, you might get some sympathetic snickers from your wife or kids, but in doing so, you've just tuned out about 70% of the listening congregation. You <u>are</u> there. It <u>is your calling</u>. You are on <u>God's</u> errand. Don't waste their time, and don't excuse yourself from performing your very best for the Lord. What's more, if you combine this excuse with the bombshell of 'what I'm about to say, you've heard before...' you're guaranteed to tune out another 29%. The 1% left listening may be your spouse (...maybe). Don't give anyone a reason to believe that what you came to share is not important, worthwhile, or beneficial for one's spiritual/emotional/social livelihood. Share instead that you are happy to have opportunity to serve our God by sharing His good word that day. If sincere, you will catch the heart of the listeners.

7. Focus your message. Sometimes you hunt with a shotgun, sometimes a rifle. Sermons can be like these hunting tools: one spreads out in a broad direction, covering a large area hoping to hit something in the general direction of the shot path; the other focuses a specific projectile toward a specific object. Sermons that touch multiple topics can have a great purpose, but should still fall under an obvious umbrella of thought. If no central theme seemingly exists to unrelated stories, the talk can 'go all over the map' and leave you audience with little to grasp. Also, the overall message of sermons with focus tends to be remembered more than messages which wander. Before your sermon, try to summarize your purpose in a single sentence. Do your scriptures, stories, illustrations, object lessons, words, all reflect this purpose?

8. Pretend each hearer who came to your sermon had to pay a $10 entrance fee. Time is the most perishable of all goods. People gladly buy tickets to hear a good musician perform, or hear a motivational speaker engage his audience. Why? Because they value the benefit derived from spending time listening to this person is worth more than the price of the ticket. While people are not 'paying' you for speaking, you are in control of that hour of their life. Is your message going to make it worth their time? Know that people are giving you something more dearly than their money—they are giving you their time. Make them not regret how they spent their hour with you.

9. Know your audience if possible. A sermon for non-members may be different than one for a pastor's retreat, for example. Knowing the spiritual/social/emotional needs of whose listening can increase your sermon's effectiveness. At the same time, yield to the Spirit. If you've had experiences with God's Spirit moving your thought process, follow it. You may be witnessing to people who need your message, whether or not you are aware.

10. Preaching by the spirit. This phrase has been known to cause some consternation in preachers. This statement, while profoundly true, does not mean you don't prepare ahead of time and does not mean you cannot make notes, if desired. Preaching by the spirit connotes more than just an impromptu message to people, hoping God steers the verbal ship instead of you. Instead, preaching 'by the Spirit' implies that God has formulated every thought and principle you share via His Spirit—and it is His thoughts that you represent and, and just mans' thought. This process can and does start well before the appointed time to speak, if we are living in the Spirit. Certainly, there are those who God said to take no thought beforehand what to say, but bear in mind he was also talking to his disciples who had lived and walked and talked with the Master. They lived in a level of the spirit that we may or may not attain. These men spent the good hours of their day (each day) in fo-

cused prayer (Acts 6). If the Spirit of God is upon you (only you can know), then you will have the mountain-top experiences—piece by piece, little by little, directing your thoughts to the sermon, talk, study, etc. You can write these down and organize them. This is not contrary to God. God said that His glory is intelligence—in other words, we also can glorify God by using the intelligence He gave you to put your thoughts in a logical pattern.

11. If you have a 'message' you really intend for people to hear—not really God—don't use a prayer as a means to encapsulate the message you really intended for people. If you've in any congregation long enough, you've probably heard it—more than once. A person's prayer (supposedly) to God contains much verbiage seemingly directed more towards the people (perhaps chastisement) than God. This is not the way to pray or to preach. Don't direct hidden messages in a prayer to a person, 'hoping' they are listening to you because you really just want to expose their flaws, faults, hoping they will 'get the point.' Never 'preach' to people during your vocal prayer. Scripture gives much better direction in dealing with interpersonal issues like these. For instance, rather than preaching through prayer, what would be more appropriate (and scripturally correct) is for the clergyman to make personal attempts to resolve conflict with the individual(s) prior to occupying the pulpit. Don't pretend to be sharing a matter with God if that isn't your 100% only reason for praying it. Think God doesn't know the difference? Prayer without real intent profits nothing but keeping God's commandments invites God's spirit to reside in power within us.

12. Discern between emotion and the spirit—within yourself. This one may sting a little because it is both sensitive and indicting. Discerning between God's Spirit and our own human emotion takes spiritual maturity. Now when the Spirit of God rests strongly on a person, human emotional expressions most certainly accompany: perhaps tears may flow, volume may increase (or decrease), and passion may swell. All of that is good if it is

'Spirit induced.' However, it is perfectly within our capability as humans to display these emotions when the spirit is <u>not</u> influencing us. This can actually happen during a sermon. Emotional responses in the absence of the Spirit can leave a listening congregation inwardly confused. It is good to be aware of the subtle differences as a speaker as well as listener.

13. Prayer and fasting is good in preparation for a sermon, but try the prayer and fasting *before* you're even asked to preach. For many, it is easier to pray and listen to the still small voice <u>before</u> a sermon assignment has been added to your workload. If you maintain regular prayer and fasting, the workload of a sermon will not be work at all. The purpose of fasting is to allow us to have a greater portion and awareness of God's Spirit. If we are in the spirit, we can be in tune with the mind and will of God. If we are in tune with God's mind and will, spiritual thoughts will abound—sermons will not be a struggle. Prepare when you don't have to! The best time to start preparing for a sermon is <u>before</u> you are asked to speak! Never get caught with the 'What am I going to speak about' blues. Keep in a daily spiritual frame of mind and your problem will not be 'what do I say?' but 'how am I going to narrow down everything the Lord has shown me!'

14. You might not need to recite every scripture you studied in preparation... Often, many scriptures support a prophetic point or spiritual principle. During ones study and preparation, one may read <u>every</u> scripture available on a particular subject. Now, the fact that you've looked them all up, highlighted and have your books' pages dog-eared to everyone, does not mean that you necessarily NEED to use EVERY ONE in your sermon. Don't misunderstand: this is not suggesting that a lot of scripture is not appropriate; rather, the point is that scripture needs to be delivered in a manner that helps the listener's mind follow the progression of thought. For instance, don't read six disjunctive passages in row without intermediate comment (for example) and expect your audience to follow your thought process. It might make sense in your head, but...Much of your

study may simply be for your spiritual preparation in order to speak on a subject. In other words, don't feel obligated to include each of the 150 verses you looked up the week before when you deliver your message. Use the ones that say it best, and people will get the idea. Besides, don't count on people to retain every verse you recite. (Now in a teaching setting, where handouts are prepared, or enough time allows the looking up many scriptures to cover a point, providing exhaustive lists is very appropriate. Just beware that in a sermon setting, an audience can be lost if many disjunctive scriptures are pasted together without enough verbal glue to hold them in the listener's mind.)

15. Make sure your sermon calls for action and response from the listeners. Good sermons offer a purpose and call the sinner to action. Not only calling for change, but offering steps to change—this is the heart of ministry—teaching application rather than reciting theory. Change might mean repentance and baptism; change could encourage mending of relationships, etc. In either case, don't just ostracize—offer guidance. Especially if this is an area you've had personal experience—for instance, when you offended someone, and then went to him/her to correct the breach. People want to, they need to hear your successes/failures if it can help them walk a more Christ-like life.

16. Don't bemoan your inadequacies as a minister for God from the pulpit. Not that we don't confess our weaknesses, but don't spend the whole talk on it. It may be appropriate to ask for prayers in your behalf, but if you've got a spiritual fence to mend with someone—mend it before you get in the pulpit. We are all weak and sinners, but if we spend all our breath expounding our faults, there comes a time when the hearers need to respect you for what you bring. You can be your own worst enemy. You don't really want the congregation rhetorically agreeing with your every personal cut down, or self-expression of inadequacy.

17. Pray John's prayer—that Jesus may increase and we may decrease (John 3:31). Don't look for personal glory from humans for your pulpit ministry. If the benefit, give God the glory. It can be hard to take a compliment if someone received ministry, but don't judge 'successes by the quantity of comments made in the foyer after your ministry. A big head is a serious spiritual handicap. Cloak your shimmering spiritual armor with the mantel of Humility.

18. Look to God's spirit for your (only) reward. Again, don't base your success on comments—quantity or quality. If you would rather trade God's reward for peoples' words, well, Jesus said 'you have your reward.' You have your reward—comment from humans rather that strength from God. Don't misunderstand—it's not bad to get good feedback either—we all inwardly desire to know that what we share can be useful to others. The issue becomes this: desire. When the purpose becomes trying to get people to 'like you' or be impressed with you, or revere you because of your God-given ability to speak publicly, you are in the first steps of diminishing your own gift.

19. Be aware of time. A noted public speaker was asked by a beginning speaker 'How to deliver a good speech to an audience.' The seasoned speaker responded 'First, you develop an attention getting introduction, then you add a dynamic conclusion...then you put them as close together in your talk as possible!' remember the adage, 'The mind can only absorb as much as the seat can endure.' Be aware of time.

20. Make eye contact—watch the non-verbal expression of your audience. You can learn to tell if they are following your thoughts. If direct eye contact feels uncomfortable, a speaker does not have to always look directly at the congregation—focusing 1-2 feet about the heads of all who are seated gives the appearance of direct eye contact and will leave the people to knowing your focus was on them and not the pulpit.

21. Use object lessons to illustrate your point. Here is an example. If you wanted to illustrate the skills one needs to be an effective witness for Christ (such as having God's word, Spirit, following his leadings, being willing to teach, etc.) you might show two fishing poles. One could be complete with rod, reel, line, lure, hook, etc.; the other may be a broken rod with no line, lure, broken reel, etc. Then compare the points of a functional fishing pole to the elements a missionary need. If one of them is missing, one may not be able to catch fish in the lake; likewise, if a spiritual principle is lacking in a missionary's life, he or she may not be able to catch souls for Christ. You get the idea. Object lessons can be very effective. While not needed for every sermon, an effective object lesson, familiar to the hearer and well taught can remain in a hearers mind for the rest of their life. Use them sparingly, but don't be afraid to use them. Every Biblical parable of Jesus contained an object lesson of various types. Know too, that object lessons will reach a wider audience—kids will get your point, not just adults.

22. Commit scripture to memory. Develop the ability to 'read' a scripture while making eye contact with your congregation. (I.E. don't make them follow the top of your head while your eyes are buried in your Bible or notes.) Sometimes an effective, non-verbal way to convey sincerity is by demonstrating your commitment to the scriptures you've selected. If you share some from memory during your talk (even paraphrased is OK), it conveys to the listener your added earnest, and simultaneously solidifies your understanding.

23. Do resolve interpersonal conflicts before you preach? In other words, don't abuse your power to captive audience and 'grind a public or personal axe' during your sermon. Unfortunately it happens: a person asked to preach has an unresolved conflict with a member of the congregation. Don't ever use your position of authority from preaching to decide to get the 'upper hand.' Don't smugly believe that no one else knows your 'hidden message' and can air dirty laundry and the pulpit will protect you. A person in this trap thinks he is getting the last

word in, but disguising it so no one else knows. While no one else may know, the person it was directed towards will know, and may resent the speaker for evermore. Again, resolve your personal conflicts before you preach. If not, you may injure someone for life.

24. Don't waste time or words. Be succinct. Pray for this ability. Mentally practice describing spiritual principles in as few words as possible. Enough said.

25. Remember, YOU Represent Jesus Christ as His appointed emissary. Look the part, speak the part. This does not require sophistry, but sincerity.

26. 'When in doubt...Don't' This means, if you share a story that may be too graphic, or embarrassing to your companion, or suggestive or in any way could make someone feel uncomfortable, if there is the least bit hesitation in sharing it, this may be a good sign not to share it at all. (For instance, don't embarrass your wife from the pulpit by telling a private health concern of hers). Also, be aware of the appropriateness of topics or examples with young children present—you don't want parents covering their children's ears in fear they will hear something 'too old' or inappropriate for them.

27. Remember the need to call sinners to make their covenant through faith, repentance and baptism according to Jesus' gospel. If not you, then who? Preaching is the basis for bringing people to Christ. You need to know the essentials of the plan of salvation, God's covenants and purpose in this world. Sort out the difference between social topics and spiritual ones. Your time behind the pulpit is God's time—be sure to use it for His case and purpose. (If the plan of salvation is a little fuzzy, look in the Appendix)

28. If it is your first time to preach—give yourself some 'pre-game' confidence. Go to the church the day before, for example, and see what it looks like to stand in the pulpit and look out on the

(empty) pews. Up till now, you may have spent your whole life comfortably looking up at the rostrum from the pews, and never had the mental picture from 'up front.' If so, don't let the first time you view the congregation from the pulpit be the first moment when you stand to begin your sermon. Even a small congregation can seem much larger than you imagined—don't psych yourself out if that view may daunt you. Go to the church ahead of time and give yourself a confidence boost.

29. Be prepared for Satan to thwart your efforts. Seems like many ministers confess they suffered their hardest week of work ever the week prior to preaching. Any coincidence? Be aware that Satan will keep your name on a bulletin board somewhere and work overtime to bod down your spiritual process. Call on God for help. You are in God's service. He can and will overcome and be victorious through you. Your public ministry can do immense good for Christ—don't let Satan's most victorious tool of despair overcome you.

30. And for the best idea, Pray that God would bless you with the great gift of preaching. This is not a 'one-time' prayer; pray it throughout the life of your ministry. Scripture records that certain individuals had such a gift of speaking the word that those who heard could not stand in their presence. Many people tend to shy away from public ministry, perhaps it's because few desire the gift. Surely, our Heavenly Father desires to bless those who seek to magnify Him through the spoken word, by outpouring His gift upon those who ask. God will answer this prayer if you desire it with all your heart.

Appendix 1

PRINCIPLES OF NON-ALIGNMENT

1. The question of when we can align with people of other faiths to accomplish a common goal is a sensitive one. How do we apply discernment in such situations?

2. For example, when is it possible to join with:
   - People of other denominations (e.g., "We may not agree on the Charismatic issue, but we do agree on the gospel, therefore we can present Christ together.")

   - People of differing faiths (e.g., "We don't agree on Christ, but we do agree that we have a common enemy in pornography, abortion, child-abuse, therefore we can fight that battle together.")

   - Or people of no religious faith at all?

3. This is what the late Dr. Francis Schaeffer called "co-belligerence", which is joint action for agreed objectives by people who disagree on other things.

4. We should evaluate all such situations carefully and proceed with caution even when no compromise is evident.

5. The best biblical principle of non-alignment is found in 2 Corinthians 6:14-7:1

    a. Don't be unequally yoked

    "Do not be bound together with unbelievers; for what partnership has righteousness and lawlessness, or what fellowship has light with darkness?"

Or what harmony has Christ with Belial, or what has a believer in common with an unbeliever? Or what agreement has the temple of God with idols? For we are the temple of the living God; just as God said, "I will dwell in them and walk among them; and I will be their God, and they shall be My people.

"Therefore, come out from their midst and be separate," says the Lord. 'And do not touch what is unclean; and I will welcome you. And I will be a father to you, and you shall be sons and daughters to Me.' Says the Lord Almighty.

"Therefore, having these promises, beloved, let us cleanse ourselves from all defilement of flesh and spirit, perfecting holiness in the fear of God."

b. In that passage Paul probably is referring to the prohibitions found in Deuteronomy 22:9-10 (see also Leviticus 19:19).

"You shall not sow your vineyard with two kinds of seed, lest all the produce of the seed which you have sown and the increase of the vineyard become defiled.

"You shall not plow with an ox and a donkey together" (because the step and pull of the two bests is unequal—they would be unequally yoked, and the task you wish to accomplish would be hindered or left undone).

c. Reinecker and Rogers comment: "The concept of the yoke was used in relation to marriage and in relation to teachers who agreed in their doctrine. A mixed marriage or cooperation with one who had a different doctrine was considered to be 'unequally yoked'"

d. That doesn't mean we are to have no contact at all with unbelievers (1 Cor 5:10), but it does mean that we are not to align or be bound with them in any way that will compromise our Christian walk or testimony.

    e. Dr. Ryre's note: "This injunction applies to marriages, business, and to ecclesiastical and intimate personal relationships."

6. Practical principle: Don't align with unbelievers in such a way as to hinder the gospel or place you in a compromising position.

7. Where the issue becomes more sensitive is when those with whom we align are professing believers whose doctrine and/or practices differ significantly from our own. In such cases, at what point does cooperation becomes compromise?

8. Here's how I deal with it:

> - I always lean toward the more conservative position because I am responsible for the church, not simply for my own opinions.
>
> - I am aware that some who disagree with my position speak of it as isolationistic, standoffish, unrealistic, divisive, and even sinful.
>
> - But my responsibility is to deal with the text of Scripture, then to make decisions accordingly to the best of my ability.
>
> - That is every believer's responsibility also.

    a. I believe that God has called us to be faithful servants of Christ and stewards of the mysteries of God (1 Cor 4:1)

    b. Paul said of himself and Timothy, "We are ambassadors for Christ, as though God were entreating through us; we beg you on behalf of Christ, be reconciled to God" (2 Cor 5:20)

c. Nothing is more important than the gospel—nothing!

- No social concern

- No political concern

- No moral concern

d. I believe that as Christians, we can and should work for moral, social, and even political reform, and those can be righteous and noble efforts if executed within biblical parameters.

e. But let us never forget that the greatest impact we have for righteous change in our families, localities, state, nation, and world, is to:
1- <u>Live a distinctively Christian life</u> (Titus 2:10).

2- <u>Train our own children in the ways of the Lord</u> (thereby transforming this generation and the next).

3- <u>And introduce lost souls to Christ</u> who will place the law of God within them and produce righteousness from the heart, not through a judicial or political system only.

f. It's a matter of priorities. Both efforts have their place, but the priority must always be to propagate the gospel.

g. Therefore, when we join with people of other faiths to achieve a common social, moral, or political goal, we must be sure that such a cooperative effort does not in any way diminish or confuse the gospel, or hinder our testimony.

h. For example:
1- I wouldn't hesitate to attend an anti-abortion rally if it were conducted within biblical and legal parameters.

2- However, I would not stand hand in hand with leaders from false religions to offer a prayer for the safe deliverance of the babies unless I could first explain
- Why I was praying,

- To whom I was praying,

- Why life is precious to God,

- That Jesus died to prevent the very thing we are rallying against,

- That regeneration, not legislation, must be our highest goal.

Otherwise we accomplish only a temporary, relative, external standard that is only as good as the popular consensus or moral consciousness of the day.

3- There are good moral reasons for preserving life of an unborn child, but beyond that, there are theological reasons, and I believe it is our privilege and responsibility to proclaim those reasons above all else.

4- Human life is sacred to God, therefore must be sacred to us, but eternal life is the far greater issue.

Therefore, we should never allow the gospel to take a back seat to any social, moral, or political issue, or to be corrupted or confused by misrepresentation.

5- It is horribly out of balance to try to save the lives of infants and not even address the greater issue of eternal life.

In the case of those who proclaim a false gospel, what a convoluted effort it is to save infants while at the same time influencing others toward the path of eternal destruction.

6- When there is no clear compromise at stake, I take each situation on its own merit, keeping in mind that abortion (for example), like every other sinful act, is a symptom and consequence of a root problem.

I believe that as Christians, we are called primarily to address the root problem, which will then eliminate the symptoms.

7- We have just so much time, energy, and resources. We must be wise and focused in how we spend them.

8- Many people fear that if all professing Christians (and even people of other faiths) don't unite against the evils of our day, sin will run rampant and ground will be lost to the Kingdom of God.

9- But God isn't suddenly impotent because our nation's sins have escalated.
- Prayer isn't suddenly useless because our nation has turned a deaf ear to God's voice.

- The God who created all things, and who raises up and brings down nations, hasn't surrendered His sovereignty.

- The God who loved the world so much that He sent His only Son to die for our sins isn't suddenly unconcerned about the elect who are still lost.

10- We must not be passive, but we must maintain our spiritual priorities.

THE BOTTOM LINE:

If I feel that the risk to the gospel is too great
- By stepping into an unequally yoked situation,
- By doing something that smacks of compromise or might bring confusion to those who see me,
- By not being able to qualify what is being said,

I choose to remain uninvolved.

If none of those things apply, then I evaluate each situation on its own merits and decide accordingly.

Appendix 2

METHODS OF ELABORATION

1. Verbal

Verbal elaboration consists of defining the words that are not completely clear, or of explaining the idioms and syntax of the grammar. There are two reasons for the need of this kind of elaboration. Our English Bible is a translation from other languages and while it is quite-reliable for all matters of doctrine, its teachings are much clearer when read in the original languages. Furthermore, our King James Version is nearly four hundred years old and contains many Arabic words which need to be explained to modern readers. For instance, Philippians 1:27 is made clearer and more interesting by explaining the word "conversation" means "citizenship." It is then seen that the following verses contain instructions regarding good Christian citizenship which applied quite appropriately to the people of Philippi who lived in a Roman Colony and who had more than average interest in citizenship. In Mark 11:24 one finds the words, "Believe that ye receive," but in elaboration it should be explained that the verb "receive" is past tense (aorist) and should read "believe that you ye have received," for the latter reading indicated a clear act of faith thus, grammar may be seen to aid elaboration. Verbal elaboration need not always be concerned with the original languages, but may be concerned also with the meanings and grammar or English words.

2. Contextual

Contextual elaboration consists of using portions of the context to throw light in the text. Usually these explanations will come from immediate context but occasionally a verse from another part of the same book will be valuable for solving a doubtful meaning. In Hebrew 12:1 the phrase, "cloud of witnesses," may be misleading if it is not interpreted in light of the preceding eleventh chapter. This reference to the context is made not alone as a matter of interpretation, but as a matter of elaboration, for it is interesting to the hearer to have familiar Scripture passages connected in a way which is not obvious on the surface.

3. Historical

Historical elaboration consists of relating historical events or conditions pertaining to the people addressed, or to the author. And elaboration of the second chapter of Colossians should include an explanation of the gnostic heresy with which certain teachers were confusing the Christians of Colosse. Philippians 1:20-25 may be partly elaborated by explaining some details of Paul's imprisonment at Rome and his impending martyrdom. Such historical and biographical data can be learned from good commentaries or Bible dictionaries.

4. Quotation of Parallel Passages

Scripture is very frequently explained by Scripture. A meager statement may be strengthened or made more lucid by the quotation of a more detailed statement of the same fact from another page of the Scriptures. Passages of doubtful import are often solved by a parallel passage which is not ambiguous. Here a word of caution is needful. Parallel passages in an expository sermon must not be more than quotations; for the exposition is of the text, not the parallel passages. One quotation can easily lead to another until the discussion is far removed from the original text.

5. Illustrations

These illustrations may come from the bible, history, experience, or modern life. By all means let there be illustrations in the expository sermon, because they make the sermon both clear and interesting. Illustrations help to avoid dryness which might characterize an expository sermon which is too largely explanation. The success of Beecher, Spurgeon, and Moody was in no small degree due to an ability to use apt illustrations. A preacher is making a mistake who does not study some good book on the art of illustrating sermons. The important thing in illustrating the expository sermon is that the illustrations be appropriated, that is, that they actually illuminate some point in the text.

6. Application

Somebody said, "Where the application begins, the sermon begins." The whole purpose of preaching is to influence men's lives and decisions by divine truth. That preachers produce Christian conversation, godly living, and brotherly love is far more important than their making admirers. That some pulpit idols will fail to gain entrance to eternal life is not entirely improbable if it is lamentable. Let us "beseech men to be reconciled to God," that we may be the worthy successors of those who "ceased not to warn everyone night and day with tears." Let it be remembered that expository sermon can be adapted to modern needs and problems and not simply a discussion of ancient people and conditions. There are two ways of making applications. They may be made along with each point in the sermon. It seems better in most cases to make the applications after each point as the sermon progresses and then to recapitulate the principle applications at the end.

Notes

References

Of God and Men by A.W. Tozer

Handbook of Preacher by Van. Cleave

Preach 118 Sermon Outlines by Anzea Publishers

Church Leader's Manual by Douglas E. Robertson

Contextualization by David J. Hasselgrave

New Testament Exposition by Walter Liefeld

God and Culture D.A. Carson and John D. Woodbridge, eds.

Spirit, Word and Story by Calvin Miller

Between Two Worlds: The Art of Preaching in the Twentieth Century by John R.W. Scott

A Voice in the Wilderness by Steve Brown, Haddon Robinson, and William Willimon

No Uncertain Sound by Donn Ketcham

Preaching Biblically: Exegesis and Interpretation by William D. Thompson

Korean Preaching by Jung Young Lee

Christian Leadership in Indian America Tom Claus and Dale Kietzman, eds.

Interpreting God's Word in Black Preaching by Warren Stewart

The Return of the Jewish Church Christianity Today by Gary Thomas

Communicating Christ Cross-Culturally by David J. Hasselgrave

Tell It Well by John T. Seamands

Dialogic Style in Preaching by George W. Swank

Reaching the Arabs by Tim Matheny

Expository Preaching for Today by Andrew Blackwood

How to Prepare Bible Messages by James Braga

Biblical Preaching by Haddon W. Robinson

The Integrity of Biblical Narrative by Mark Ellingsen

Preach On! by J. Alfred Smith

Christ-Centered Preaching by Brian Chappell

Theories of Preaching: Selected Readings in the Homiletical Tradition by Richard Lischer

Christ's Preaching and Ours by Michael Philibert

Study of Non-Verbal Communication by Thomas Chadwick

Inductive Preaching by Ralph Lewis and Gregg Lewis

Learning to Preach Like Jesus by Ralph Lewis and Greg Lewis

The Crisis in Expository Preaching Today" Preaching by Walter C. Kaiser

Scripture, Tradition, and Interpretation W.W. Gasque and W.S. Lasor, eds.

Liberation Theology and Hermeneutical Preunderstandings by Larry D. Petegrew

Man as Male and Female by Paul K. Jewett

New Testament Interpretation I. Howard Marshall, ed.

Missiology: An International Review by Haleblian Krikor

Introduction to Exegesis by Robert L. Thomas

Bible Translations: The Link between Exegesis and Expository Preaching by The Master's Seminary Journal

Improving Evangelical Ethics: An Analysis of the Problem and a Proposed Solution by Robert L. Thomas

Toward a Science of Translation by Eugene A. Nida

Bible Translations for Popular Use by William L. Wonderly

Exegetical Fallacies by D.A. Carson

New Hermeneutic by Thiselton

Feminist Interpretation of the Bible Letty M. Russell, ed.

Doing Theology in a Revolutionary Situation by J. M. Bonino

Culture and Super Culture, Practical Anthropology 2 by William A. Smalley

Christianity in Culture by Charles H. Kraft

The Origins of New Testament Christology by I. Howard Marshall

The Anatomy of Preaching by David L. Larsen

In the Biblical Preacher's Workshop by Dwight E. Stevenson

On the Preparation and Delivery of Sermons by John A. Broadus; Revised by Rev. Vernon L. Stanfield

Expository Preaching Without Notes by Charles W. Koller

Principles of Expository Preaching by Merrill F. Unger

The Tests of Life by Robert Law

The New Testament in its Library Environment by David E. Aune

Literary Approaches to Biblical Interpretation by Tremper Longman, III

The Bible in the Pulpit: The Renewal of Biblical Preaching by Leander E. Keck

The Modern Preacher and the Ancient Text by Sidney Greidanus

Thoughts on Preaching by James W. Alexander

Principles and Practice of Preaching by Ilion T. Jones

Power in Expository Preaching by Faris D. Whitesell

The Preacher and His Models by James Stalker

The Supremacy of God in Preaching by John Piper

Preaching With Power the Word "Correctly Handled" to Transform Man and His World by Louis Goldberg

The Infallible World (3rd Edition) Paul Wooley ed.

A Plea for Expository Preaching by Greer W. Boyce

Expository Preaching Plans and Methods by F. B. Meyer

The Art of Effective Preaching by William W. Ayer

Hermeneutics, Exegesis, and Proclamation Criswell Theological Review

Toward An Exegetical Theology by Jerry Vines and David Allen

Protestant Bible Interpretation (3rd Revised Edition) by Bernard Rann

Principles and Practice of Greek Exegesis by John D. Grassmick

Essentials for Biblical Preaching by Al Fasol

The Preacher's Portrait by John R. W. Scott

Homiletics: The Art and Science of Preaching by Pastor Art Kohl

Power in the Pulpit by Jerry Vines and Jim Saddix

Preparing Expository Sermons by Ramesh Richard

Rediscovering Expository Sermons by Richard Mayhue

Lectures to My Students by Charles Haddon Spurgeon

Preaching and Preachers by D. Martyn Lloyd-Jones

Webster's Ninth New Collegiate Dictionary by Merriam-Webster

What Is Expository Preaching? by Hadden W. Robinson

INDEX

Bible v, 3, 7, 10, 19, 23, 39, 41, 42, 44, 45, 47, 48, 49, 53, 55, 56, 57, 58, 59, 60, 61, 63, 64, 65, 66, 69, 71, 72, 73, 74, 76, 77, 78, 81, 82, 83, 84, 85, 86, 87, 88, 89, 90, 92, 94, 97, 100, 103, 119, 123, 125, 126, 127, 129, 131, 133, 134, 138, 141, 144, 148, 149, 152, 153, 155, 164, 175, 176, 184, 185, 186

exegesis 55, 56, 58, 60, 78, 81, 82, 84, 85, 86, 87, 88, 89, 90, 91, 100, 102, 104, 105, 138, 139

Exposition 55, 65, 81, 82, 86, 88, 89, 90, 94, 101, 183

expositional 55, 75

Homiletics 39, 87, 186

preacher 2, 5, 10, 39, 40, 43, 50, 54, 55, 57, 58, 59, 60, 61, 62, 63, 64, 70, 71, 72, 76, 78, 82, 89, 90, 91, 92, 93, 94, 95, 97, 98, 99, 100, 101, 102, 105, 112, 116, 118, 119, 130, 132, 133, 134, 136, 137, 139, 140, 141, 143, 145, 149, 150, 155, 156, 176

Preaching i, iii, v, 5, 6, 40, 48, 55, 56, 57, 61, 63, 69, 73, 75, 76, 78, 79, 81, 92, 97, 100, 101, 130, 132, 138, 139, 141, 143, 154, 155, 159, 165, 183, 184, 185, 186

sermon delivery 154

sermon preparation 39, 77, 78, 81, 87, 89, 91, 98, 139

sermons 1, 6, 7, 9, 10, 11, 39, 46, 48, 49, 57, 61, 72, 79, 81, 93, 97, 98, 103, 114, 121, 123, 126, 128, 129, 131, 132, 133, 138, 143, 150, 155, 158, 161, 162, 176

study 7, 9, 24, 42, 45, 46, 56, 58, 59, 62, 69, 70, 71, 72, 82, 84, 86, 90, 92, 100, 101, 132, 134, 140, 149, 155, 160, 161, 176

transition 2, 89, 90, 117, 118

Transition 2, 107, 110, 111, 112, 117, 118

Transitions 1

www.ingramcontent.com/pod-product-compliance
Lightning Source LLC
Chambersburg PA
CBHW021137300426
44113CB00006B/464